ADDRESSING THE DUAL CAREER
DILEMMA WITH CARE

WHOSE CAREER

YOURS,
MINE
OR OURS?

YVONNE QUAHE

Disclaimer

Permissions have been sought in regard to any copyrighted materials included in this book where possible and every attempt has been made to contact the copyright owners. Some names, locations and identifying features have been changed to preserve the anonymity of the people involved.

Praise for *Whose Career – Yours, Mine or Ours?*

"Yvonne Quahe has written an essential book for professional couples. Her insights will help you navigate challenging personal and professional questions, and make the decisions that are right for you and your family."

Dorie Clark
Duke and Columbia Business Professor
Top 50 Business Thinkers in the World – *Thinkers50*
#1 Communication Coach in the World – Marshall Goldsmith
Leading Global Coaches Awards
"An expert in self-reinvention and helping others make changes in their lives." – *The New York Times*

"An essential guide for everyone on an international dual-career journey, whether starting out or on your umpteenth move. Yvonne Quahe has walked this path herself and The CARE Code and real-life stories will help you work through the challenges and see a landscape of possibilities."

Kathleen van der Wilk-Carlton
Founder and Board Member, Permits Foundation

"This book is a real gift to couples who want to think generatively, productively and deliberately about their future careers together. I read it in one sitting and drew inspiration from the case studies, the practical tools and most importantly, the lessons learnt by all the contributors along the way. My only regret – the fact that this book wasn't available when I embarked on my own dual career!"

Samantha Rockey
Co-founder and Director of Thompson Harrison 'Helping Leaders Do What Matters Most.'
Associate Fellow, SAID Business School, Oxford University

"As a very young child, my commercial banking father was relocated to Asia for work. We all came along, of course. My mother was the quintessential stay-at-home wife, mother and author with a live-in housekeeper and babysitter. It was the 1970s when women weren't expected to work. Today, we are attracted to like-minded brains and adventurers. Yvonne Quahe has carefully provided couples in the 2020s with the thinking, approach and behaviors we need if we are to create the rich professional and personal adventures we seek with our most significant other. A must-read."

Caroline Stokes
CEO, FORWARD
Author of *Elephants Before Unicorns: Emotionally Intelligent Strategies To Save Your Company*

"It was a pleasure to read Yvonne's personal story about how she and her husband tackled the many challenges of a Dual Career Couple. The case studies added substance and affirmation to a variety of suggested approaches to preserve careers and family life. This is a great read that should be required reading for couples considering a move!"

Craig B. Toedtman
Founder & CEO, Resource Development Company, Inc.
www.rdcinc.com

"One day you will tell your story of how you've overcome what you are going through now and it will become part of someone else's survival guide."

Ehraz Ahmed
Founder and CEO of Aspirehive

To Graham
My G.O.A.T.

Contents

Foreword..i
What You Will Find in This Book..iii
Introduction...ix

PART ONE – UNDERSTANDING
THE DUAL CAREER DILEMMA

Chapter 1 – In the Beginning:
My Dual Career Story

My Dual Career Story 1
Reality Dawns 1
Dual Career Conversations..12
Points for Reflection...16

Chapter 2 – Dual Career Couples
and International Relocation

and International Relocation...17
I Didn't Want To, But… 17
The Conundrum That Won't Go Away:
Career Prioritization and the Dual Career Couple 20
A Punishing Landscape for the Partner....................................22
Enter the Great Disruptors..24
Mitigating the Disruptors..31
Points for Reflection...37

Chapter 3 – The Professional Follower

Chapter 3 – The Professional Follower 39
The Accompanying Partner Syndrome 39
What the Partners Say 41
What Are the Issues? 49
What Happens to Accompanying Partners on International
Assignments?...51
Are You Following Along? 53
Can We Create a Win for All? 54
Points for Reflection...56

Chapter 4 – A Win for All: The Career Stories of Six Couples 57

Case Study 1: Turn-Taking – Robert and Rosemary 61
Case Study 2: Double Primary – Melissa and Christian...........67
Case Study 3: Primary-Secondary – Maja and Henrik 74
Case Study 4: Role Reversal – Amanda and Simon..................82
Case Study 5: Combination of Turn-Taking,
Primary-Secondary and Role Reversal – Cielo and Charles.......92
Case Study 6: Non-Traditional, Same-Sex Couple
– Chuck and Chen..98
What Can We Learn about Successful Dual Careers
from These Case Studies?..102
Points for Reflection 105

PART TWO – APPLYING THE CARE CODE TO ADDRESS THE DILEMMA

Chapter 5 – Putting CARE into the Dual Career 107

Why Have CARE Conversations? 107
What Is a CARE Conversation? 108
The Seeds of The CARE Code...109
The CARE Code 113
How to Have a CARE Conversation 117
Essentials for CARE Conversations 118
Exercises to Kickstart Your CARE Conversations 121

Chapter 6 – How Organizations Can CARE 137

What Can We Learn from Research?......................................137
Why Is the Old Model Not Working? 141
What Can Organizations Do? 143

Chapter 7 – Conclusion: Keeping Your Focus on CARE 149

Staying on Track..149
CARE Makes It Work 150

Quick Reference Guide 152
Resources 157
Acknowledgments 169
About the Author 171

Foreword

I first met Yvonne Quahe in Singapore where we were introduced by mutual friends. At the time, I was living in Yvonne's hometown as an expatriate and university lecturer and she was living in Washington DC (where she still lives) as a professional expatriate working for the World Bank. Our paths crossed because we are both passionate about the same field – global dual-career families. Fast forward a few years and we have remained in touch on a regular basis, sometimes in person when Yvonne has been visiting home, but mostly on FaceTime and WhatsApp. Our conversations are frequently long and detailed, during which we share a lot of research and swap ideas. Yvonne has been a willing sounding board on many of my publications and studies as much as I have been hers for programs and projects she is rolling out for her organization. Our dialogue about dual careers has always (ALWAYS!) been honest and raw. We have each lived the life (for decades) and know deep within our souls that irreverence and anecdotes serve no one.

In this book, Yvonne speaks her truth not just for herself but (more importantly) for the many thousands of other dual-career expatriate spouses living around the world. This is a book about the hard reality of expatriate life for an accompanying partner who is following their spouse or partner's career abroad. Without any doubt, it is a tough life. To outsiders, such a life might appear to be full of glamour and exoticness, and while there are moments of that to be sure, much of the dual-career expatriate life is an extremely challenging inner journey that most people around us don't see. It can be incredibly lonely, soul-destroying, humiliating, and even marriage-ending (which Yvonne and I have seen many times). It can also be life-changing, deeply affirming, spectacularly exciting and even career-enhancing. My research, coupled with Yvonne's decades of on-the-ground experience, attests that it is a roller-coaster ride not meant for the faint-hearted, on which many embark and few truly achieve a successful outcome. In the pages of this book, Yvonne takes the reader through all of it. Using case studies that reflect the real-life complexities that all dual-career expatriate couples face, we are exposed to the twists and turns of decision-making and how couples cope (and pivot) when jobs and careers turn out to be less satisfying than first hoped.

Yvonne is a tireless advocate for helping people overcome dual-career challenges. In her many years of professional experience in this field, she has brought positive change to an area of global mobility that is at best overlooked and at worst dismissed as irrelevant. Still, she fights on.

I have written this foreword because Yvonne asked me to. However, that does not mean I automatically said yes. As a leading expert on global mobility, I am approached several times a year to write forewords and provide recommendations for books about global families. My standard reply is that I do not endorse non-academic work as it rarely meets the rigor and deep insight that academic work demands and on which I have built my academic credibility. In Yvonne's case, I have made an exception. That is how passionate I am about not only the subject matter but the way in which she has tackled it.

If you have bought this book, you are in safe hands. I say that with confidence and a deep conviction that this book has the potential to be a game changer.

Dr. Yvonne Kallane (McNulty)
Perth, Australia
June 2021

Author of
Working Internationally: Expatriates, Migrants and Other Global Workers
The Research Handbook of Expatriates
The Research Handbook of Globally Mobile Families

What You Will Find in This Book

This book is based not only on my own 30-plus years of experience as an Accompanying Partner, living in multiple overseas locations, but also on my extensive experience in global mobility and partner support, latterly specializing in Dual Career Couples. In addition to this, I have conducted extensive research into the topic, and read and studied widely. Lastly, having worked closely with hundreds of globally mobile Dual Career Couples, I have had the privilege of being able to interview them and conduct personal research, which has provided me with both anecdotal and diagnostic evidence in this field.

Beyond short anecdotal examples, the book presents six detailed Case Studies that describe the achievements and challenges of Dual Career Couples. Although these couples had different priorities, they adopted similar techniques to maintain harmony within their relationship as they sought to fulfill their plans. Based on extensive research and a close examination of these success stories (as well as my own), I have developed The CARE Code. The focus of The CARE Code is on providing you with a framework for systematic dialogue that will guide you through the Dual Career challenges you face as a couple.

This book is called *Whose Career – Yours, Mine or Ours?* because all too often one career takes precedence over the other and the concept of a Dual Career marriage disintegrates into dust. Your career decisions should be made jointly and work for both of you. Marriage is, after all, a partnership.

Yes, the essence of this book is about partnership. Its primary focus is on Dual Career Couples having conversations about how they are going to make their Dual Careers work for them as a couple and/or family in the context of being globally mobile. However, once the couple have clarity about how to navigate their career paths and support each other, the other key stakeholders for traditional expatriates are the organizations they work for.

Organizations have not always recognized that, for Dual Career Couples, the partner's career needs to be factored into any plans for international assignments. Providing an attractive package in the new location is no longer a sufficient enticement, and companies are in danger of losing their top talent unless they take steps to resolve this dilemma. I provide some suggestions for organizations to consider.

In the pages that follow, I will share what I have learned about the benefits and disadvantages of being in a Dual Career partnership and, most importantly, how to give both partners' professional ambitions the best possible chance of success.

PART ONE – UNDERSTANDING THE DUAL CAREER DILEMMA sets the scene and gives you the facts. This section is all about us, the people like you and me involved in a Dual Career partnership. Along the way you will come across a series of Eight Golden Rules that you can apply throughout your Dual Career journey, as well as Twelve Common Pitfalls to avoid. Each of the four chapters in this section ends with a space where you can write your own reflections on the content that resonates with you. You may want to use this to spark a discussion with your partner.

In *Chapter 1, In the Beginning*, I outline my own career story complete with the naivety and mistakes that colored the first few years. I know my story resonates with many, and my research proves it is typical. This is where I introduce you to the idea that having Dual Career Conversations is crucial.

In *Chapter 2, Dual Career Couples and International Relocation*, it's time to look closely at the many issues faced by partners, particularly when an international assignment beckons, and consider ways to mitigate them.

In *Chapter 3, The Professional Follower*, I head to the experts and published research from authors, surveys and articles, as well as to my own research, to show the current Dual Career landscape and what that means for today's partners.

Chapter 4, A Win for All, shares in-depth Case Studies of six couples who have navigated the Dual Career landscape effectively. You will find inspiration and resonance within their stories. In addition, I have identified the common denominators and elements that have led to Dual Career success for these couples.

PART TWO – APPLYING THE CARE CODE TO ADDRESS THE DILEMMA provides a framework and exercises that can help you (both individually and as a couple) define your priorities and have productive conversations as you steer your way through the issues and challenges facing every Dual Career Couple. Since the organization you work for is a key stakeholder, one chapter is devoted to the role it can play in enabling you, as a couple, to achieve satisfaction in your professional careers.

Chapter 5, Putting CARE into the Dual Career, explains how you can use The CARE Code (Clarify, Assess, Refocus, Explore) to have effective Dual Career Conversations as a couple. The guidance on these conversations includes five exercises that will help you to understand your individual priorities and make the discussions with your partner productive and less fraught. These exercises do not have to be done sequentially; they are designed to be helpful throughout your Dual Career discussions and can be revisited regularly as required. A sixth exercise is included to help you prepare for a career conversation with HR or your line manager.

Chapter 6, How Organizations Can CARE, uses the research on Dual Career Couples as the rationale for organizations needing to rethink their talent management strategy. It also provides suggestions on what organizations can do to retain talented staff whose partners also have career ambitions.

Chapter 7, Conclusion: Keeping Your Focus on CARE, clarifies how you can stay on track and make sure the good habits you have developed, such as productive career conversations, remain a feature of your relationship.

In a nutshell, I explain how to manage Dual Career dilemmas and international moves successfully – without resentment and without committing career suicide. To achieve this, I show how The CARE Code can help Dual Career Couples discuss and navigate their individual and joint objectives. The CARE Code can be used by HR and/or global mobility professionals when discussing international moves with talented staff who may be reluctant to move because of joint career ambitions.

Who Is the Book For?

This book is called *Whose Career – Yours, Mine or Ours?* because Dual Career success is elusive unless the couple develop an 'OUR' mindset. Juggling two careers, multiple moves and perhaps a family is complex, and there is no one-size-fits-all solution. Better career and life decisions are made when the couple clarify what matters to them and jointly explore how to make it work for 'us.' This book is primarily for:

- Dual Career Couples who are considering a global assignment and want to explicitly discuss the impact of international assignments on career continuation.

- Dual Career Couples who want to thrive in both their careers and their life as a family.

- The professional follower who has decided 'it will be my turn next' or wishes to renegotiate career prioritization in their relationship.

- The Accompanying Partner who may not have worked for some years but is keen to explore opportunities for retraining and/or a career change.

- Dual Career Couples on rotation and on the brink of having to decide 'where to' next.

- Human Resources and/or global mobility professionals looking for tools to help talent mobility.

- Any Dual Career Couple who want to develop an 'our' mindset.

Introduction

One hot, humid April afternoon in Manila, my Australian friend Valerie and I were sitting under the gentle hum of the ceiling fan and sipping fresh, ice-cold lime juice. Valerie tipped her head a little closer to mine and said in a low whisper, "Guess what, Yvonne? Now I've only gone and contracted a sexually transmitted disease."

It was commonly known that her husband was going through a midlife crisis, frequenting seedy bars and the like.

"Just leave him!" I responded quickly, never one to beat about the bush and both horrified and indignant by turn that my friend should suffer such a fate.

"What do you suggest I do once I leave him?" she volleyed back without hesitation. "I gave up my profession 20 years ago to follow him around the world; I don't even know where my home is."

I was about to come up with some suggestions, but something inside me told me to 'shut up' because, in truth, finding a solution could be like finding a needle in a haystack. Valerie had been out of the job market for two decades. She was enjoying a life of leisure – there was a housemaid and a driver – but was in a predicament. It was as if she had become a 'professional follower.' It was interesting to me that although Valerie was a very resourceful person, she felt emotionally unable to make a stand for herself. Was this caused by years of eroding self-confidence and a lack of financial independence? She kept punctuating our conversation with the repeated question, "Where shall I go?"

In that moment, I made a vow that, to the extent that it was within my capabilities, I would not see this happen to me or any other woman. That day the seeds of my interest, advocacy and eventually my expertise in Dual Careers were sown. But this is not just about women. Men too find themselves in this position of feeling trapped. Both men and women can be affected like this if they, like Valerie, have been an 'Accompanying Partner,' or a term often deridingly called 'trailing spouse.'

In reality, women take the brunt of 'following' their partners. Although the number of women on global assignments has increased over the years, the Relocating Partner Survey by EY and NetExpat (2018) shows that 71% of international assignees are still male.

Moreover, nearly 80% of women and 70% of men cite partner unwillingness to move because of career as the main reason for not accepting an international assignment. The reality is more nuanced; the assumption that career privilege is the male's prerogative is slowly changing. Many a woman has assumed that she has to give up her job and 'follow' her husband. Most women, however, do not assume that their partner will give up his job to follow her; they are more consultative about the decision to go or may even reject the assignment because they assume their partner won't be willing to move.

My Danish friend Annette and I were having a drink one evening discussing how to grow her fledgling consultancy business. She explained that she was once offered a position in Mexico but turned it down.

"Why ever did you do that?" I asked, incredulous that she would say no.

Annette continued, "It required living on a compound out in a remote area of Mexico and I just knew Andreas would not cope."

"Did you ask him?" I asked, curious to know how they made that decision.

"No," she said, "I assumed he wouldn't want to go and I didn't think he would cope in that particular environment anyway." In the twinkling of an eye, she had turned down what could have been a great career opportunity for her.

No one needs to 'follow' anyone. The decisions have to be co-owned by both partners. Career prioritization has to be discussed between the couple, openly and honestly. It is challenging enough to make two careers work when you are living in one place, let alone when you factor in international mobility and moving from country to country every three to five years. Many couples just assume that it will all work out because they love each other. As one newly arrived partner told me blithely, "We believe I'll find a job in DC." With people being made redundant daily due to the Covid-19 pandemic, this seemed a little incongruous. Life is more complicated. Only ostriches believe in a fairy-tale ending.

Finding Your Voice

When will my turn come? Didn't we agree that both our careers were equally important?

Have you said this before? I know I have.

While some Accompanying Partners have thrived as they have moved around the world, others remain angry at being the victims of the 'winner takes it all' syndrome. The lead partner 'wins' and the Accompanying Partner 'loses' time and again. Others, after years of dealing with resentment, come to realize that not being the main breadwinner is not so bad after all and find rebirth in new possibilities. This rebirth can be a long time coming, sometimes taking 10 to 15 years. The toll of not speaking up, or not speaking clearly soon enough, weighs heavy, leading to marital tension, loss of self-confidence and lack of personal fulfillment.

I find it curious that some Accompanying Partners keep their mouths shut, never expressing their fury and frustration to their partner. They talk about it to friends, at expatriate coffee mornings, to their coaches and counselors, but rarely to their partner.

"Have you ever had a Dual Career Conversation with your partner?" I ask them when they visit me in my office.

"Dual Career Conversation? What's that?" Fatou says, staring at me blankly.

"Don't you discuss your career decisions with your partner?" I reply. Although I must have asked this question hundreds of times, I never fail to be shocked by their incredulous response.

"No, it is always going to be his career before mine," she shoots back. "Never crossed my mind to discuss it. Besides, I can't speak to him about it," she continues as we head in the direction of the coffee bar for a coaching conversation.

Fatou takes a seat at a corner table and stirs a spoonful of sugar into her latté before turning to look at me quizzically. It's as if she is trying to read my mind. I take a sip of my own long-awaited latté and wait.

"It's not going to happen that way, is it?" she starts.

"No," I begin, fighting the desire to sigh. "It will have to be crafted by both of you together. Think of it as a kind of dance. Like the tango, it takes two. You both have to agree to the kind of 'dance' you want to do and then work out the steps. Together. Over time, the music may change, or you may prefer another type of dance. What matters is that both partners agree on the steps *and* the new dance each time."

It is the many conversations like this that made me consider how I can help couples have these important discussions. Frank, open communication between a couple is the essence of a healthy relationship. Lesley Lewis, an American-Brit who has spent many decades in Hong Kong working as a psychologist and therapist, has worked with countless expatriate couples during her 40-plus years of practice. She knows the issues.

"The three main causes of relationship breakdown are money, sex and communication," she says. "Many couples never take the time to discuss any of them. Having Dual Career Conversations doesn't cross their minds."

I have been an internationally mobile spouse all my working life; over 30 years. Born in Singapore, life and mostly the career of my British husband, Graham, have taken us around the world to Hong Kong, Singapore, the Philippines, England, and now Washington DC, in the United States. I have always been fiercely protective of my career and yet, even for me, I've found myself enabling him to take the lead and to 'win' for the first few years of our mobile life. Once that changed, I made it my life's work to help other Accompanying Partners to take their professional life off the back burner. Even if you haven't made joint decisions before, it is never too late to change or recalibrate.

Join me on the journey of discovery, enter into the stories of Anjana, Jawara and Hao, and many more; you may see your own story reflected in pieces of their stories. Walk with me through the common pitfalls that we inadvertently fall into, the challenges of international mobility and its impact on Dual Career Couples. These are stories of challenge and success. More importantly, learn to use the CARE Code to guide your conversations as you discuss the answer to *Whose Career – Yours, Mine or Ours?* It is a question you will need to revisit many times over the course of conscious coupling. Proceed with CARE.

Yvonne Quahe
MA in Leading Innovation and Change
Certificate in Brain-Based Coaching
www.yvonnequahe.com

Washington DC
July 2021

PART ONE

UNDERSTANDING THE DUAL CAREER DILEMMA

Chapter 1

In the Beginning:
My Dual Career Story

In this chapter you will learn:

- Is it even possible to be a Dual Career expatriate?
- What elements are required to make your Dual Career life have a chance?

Reality Dawns

It is hard to believe how badly we had managed our expectations more than 30 years ago when my British husband, Graham, and I were in the early years of our careers. I had a degree in Sociology and two years of work experience as a personal assistant, which I loathed. Coming from Singapore, as I do, being a high achiever was all I knew. Beyond that solitary ambition, I was fairly clueless as to how to go about forging a meaningful career for myself, though I knew I fancied being a journalist. In the end I did what the Career Services recommended most women graduates did at the time – I became the personal assistant to a chief executive. I hated every minute of it. Graham had found a job in Brighton on the south coast of England and so that was where we began our newly-married life. He was teaching at a private school and was as nonplussed as me about our individual career possibilities, let alone as a career couple. Still, we had to start somewhere. Already I had taken a back seat and I had not even noticed.

Our first move

The phone on my desk rang to break the boredom of another dull and drizzly day at the office. It was Graham. I was always happy to hear his voice but also a little worried as he never normally called during work hours. In low whispers, clearly worried that someone might hear, he began to speak.

"I think it's time I quit and move on. Can you get all the information you can on courses for me?" *Click*. The phone went down as suddenly as the call had begun.

It never fails to surprise me how quickly a mundane landscape can suddenly change into a treasure trove waiting to be discovered and explored. Almost at once, I was no longer the bored personal assistant to the academic director of Brighton Polytechnic, but a secret agent tasked with finding the loot.

My common sense told me that I should find courses in languages and linguistics, given his academic and professional background. I scoured the library, files and brochures with newfound zest and energy, photocopying the relevant information.

GOLDEN RULE #1: SHARE CAREER UPS AND DOWNS WITH YOUR PARTNER; IT'S NOT 'YOURS' AND 'MINE' – IT'S 'OURS'

That evening after dinner we carefully pored over the information. Again, common sense prevailed. Why not study Teaching English as a Foreign Language (TEFL)? After all it was and still is the most widely learned second language. Moreover, English is either the official or one of the official languages of almost 60 sovereign states. Armed with this qualification, the world would be our oyster.

We patted ourselves on the back for resolving this so quickly and Graham then put his mind to applying for the courses that appealed to him.

◉ GOLDEN RULE #2: MAKE SHARED DECISIONS

In due course, Graham was offered a place at the University of Kent to pursue a postgraduate course in Teaching English as a Foreign Language. Reluctantly, I allowed my own dreams to come second and resigned from my job. I wasn't happy there after all, so what did it matter? It's only as I write this today, years later, that I realize we had inadvertently set in motion the 'Accompanying Partner syndrome.' I had been genuinely engaged in the process that refocused my husband's career, yet, at the same time, I had been willingly but unknowingly digging my own career grave. I put it down to not knowing what I really wanted to do, which made following Graham the easy option.

⚇ COMMON PITFALL #1: LETTING YOUR CAREER COME SECOND TOO EASILY

Once he had that postgraduate qualification in TEFL under his belt, we could start applying for jobs abroad (note how I used the personal pronoun 'we'). Graham wanted to cement his credentials as a language specialist and I, now listless in my own career journey, fell into step behind him. We were only in Canterbury for one academic year, so again I found myself doing something I didn't much like, this time for Age Concern. At least it kept me busy.

These were pre-internet days, so every Friday evening one of us would stop by our friendly newsagent, Hugh, a retired ex-colleague of Graham's, to collect *The Times Higher Education Supplement* to scour the jobs' pages. Experience was what he needed to supplement his qualifications and so he applied for jobs as near as Hillingdon in London, to Hong Kong on the other side of the world, while completing his thesis.

We waited anxiously every day for the post. I was late coming home from work one day and was busy rustling up a quick pasta supper. Graham was strangely absorbed, I thought, but I brushed it aside without much thought as we were both hungry and in need of dinner. Sitting down at our dining table, he picked up his fork and looked over to the stove where I was ladling his favorite Bolognese sauce.

"I know you have something to tell me," I began. "You look a bit shifty. Should I be sitting down?" I laid our blue and white rice pattern Chinese bowls on the table. Was this the moment we had been waiting for?

He could not contain himself and before he'd even had his first mouthful, he blurted, "I got the job in Hong Kong!" Seven words that would change our lives forever.

I couldn't contain my excitement. Of all the jobs he (we!) had applied for, this was the one I hoped he would get. This was it. It was actually happening.

What could be more exhilarating than leaving the grey skies of England behind and heading toward home? As a Singaporean, Hong Kong was closer to my roots. Christmas at 'home' was already booked. We'd agreed early on that we'd never go to Singapore unless our careers took us there, so this seemed like the best of both worlds. We both had bags of ambition, together with huge excitement and expectation.

◎ GOLDEN RULE #3: SET YOUR 'NO-GO' AREAS
   EARLY ON

We arrived in Kowloon, Hong Kong, on a sweltering afternoon in late August. After the quiet towns on the south coast of England, I had completely forgotten what it was like to have beads of perspiration trickling from your forehead to your feet as you navigated your way through the hustle and bustle of a congested city. We were given a tiny flat on campus. It was built into the hillside, so it only had windows on one side. What happened to the balcony with views of the harbor? Graham could hardly stretch his arm out in the bathroom. The contrast with our postgraduate accommodation in the leafy cul-de-sac outside the city walls of Canterbury was stark. We had sold our car, rented out our flat and stored the remainder of our belongings in his parents' loft. There was no turning back. We were here and ready to get stuck in. Swiftly it became my job to help us settle in. I took to it with some trepidation mixed with enthusiasm, and the time passed quickly.

It was a matter of weeks before we discovered our contract wasn't quite what it seemed and decided we would leave after the academic year was up.

It seemed silly for me to try and find a decent job for such a short time and so I decided I might as well teach English to a range of students, from rich Hong Kong socialites to ambitious professionals, 'just to fill my time.' I didn't much like the work, but it was amusing for a while and gave me something to do. I had naturally fallen upon two common strategies Accompanying Partners use to find work. Without realizing it, I had simply made a decision to sell something that customers wanted. At the time, it felt like a random decision. I had no training in Teaching English as a Foreign Language – unlike my husband – but I didn't let that stop me.

Like I said, I was fumbling in the dark. Did I have any training? No! Did it seem to matter? Not a jot. Sometimes confidence and self-belief can get you just as far as qualifications or experience.

Sometimes being a 'big fish in a small pond' is all it takes for you to see success in an area you would never normally entertain.

COMMON PITFALL #2: MAKING DO WITH WHAT IS AT HAND RATHER THAN FOCUSING ON YOUR CAREER PATH

Little did I know, the die was cast, and I would tumble into doing what is easily at hand many more times in the next few years – almost by accident. My 'real' career could wait. There was no way I wanted to teach English forever, but it would do for now. Does this sound familiar?

Having decided not to stay in his job, Graham found himself another position, this time at the Singapore Polytechnic: my home country. I was delighted; I would be going home and the sky was the limit as far as career was concerned.

Going 'home'

And so, a year later, on another sticky, humid August afternoon, we arrived in Singapore. I was excited about the freedom I would have to pursue my longed-for career of being a journalist. Sure, I had no qualifications in this either, but since I had dreams, enthusiasm and ideas, I didn't let that stop me. I approached *The Straits Times* in the hope of an opportunity. My hopes were quickly dashed.

I discovered that one of the conditions of training meant I would be entitled to just 14 working days' vacation a year! Worse, I would have to work on Saturdays. I was devastated. It is hard to describe the potent mix of disappointment, frustration and conflicting emotions that arise when competing priorities surface. The tension of my competing interests left me with a hollow feeling deep in my gut. So often, sadly, Dual Career Conversations between partners can resemble a tug-of-war. Of course, I vented my frustration in our many discussions. "Is life so unfair?" became the signature tune of every dinner conversation, like an unending broken record.

The truth was that we knew we would not be in Asia forever and would return to England before long. Naturally, we wanted to travel, to explore the region. Graham, an academic, had wonderfully long holidays. How was that going to work if I had a measly two weeks a year? It was only our second posting and our careers seemed totally incompatible for a reason that had never crossed our minds. I was in my home country, where I was supposed to have an advantage. We just did not know how to balance this tension. Clearly, love and communication weren't enough.

COMMON PITFALL #3: SOON YOUR TWO CAREERS ARE OUT OF SYNC

The first hurdle

Enter our first major Dual Career hurdle: How could I align our careers, values and interests? How much did I want to pursue my own career ambitions, and at what cost? And how important was it to take advantage of the opportunities to travel within the region that both of us had always wanted to do?

COMMON PITFALL #4: COMPETING PRIORITIES GET IN THE WAY

Suddenly, I felt bereft, like a child forcefully separated from her mother. The dream of going 'home,' where everything will be alright, was in smithereens. How could the promised land have failed me so badly? This question was never far from me. It stuck to me like a rash; an itch that never went away. I would have no visa or work permit restrictions. I had contacts and networks.

I should have been able to do what I wanted. Now my dreams were in jeopardy. What choices would I make?

It's *our* life

In the end, I chose 'our' life, aka, 'his' life. In other words, I agreed to fall into step behind Graham. Again, I settled for teaching English as a second language at a polytechnic because it would give us similar breaks so we could pursue our travels. And travel we did: short weekends away and longer trips to Hawaii, Australia and New Zealand during the longer vacations. I did what I could to salvage the career dream that had not had the chance to leave the starting blocks and wrote a shopping column for *The Straits Times*, despite having no experience or training.

I had something else on my side – I came from a well-known local family. My maternal grandfather was the first Western-educated eye surgeon in Singapore and his wife, my maternal grandmother, of Indonesian-Chinese heritage, was one of the first Asian women to graduate from university in the USA. They were of a class and breed who can be considered pioneers. In short, I was a big fish in a small pond. A publisher had read my articles in *The Straits Times* and soon I was commissioned to write and publish a book on the social history of the pioneers of Singapore using oral history as the method of documentation. He thought that as the granddaughter of Dr Lim Eng Hae, I would have access to personal interviews to many of the pioneers who were contemporaries of my grandfather. Soon the obituary page of *The Straits Times* became the first page I turned to every morning. I never enjoyed the teaching. If I am truthful, I hated it. Somehow, I managed to straddle both worlds, keeping the pilot light of my dreams on a low flicker. However, any feeling of fulfillment continued to escape me.

The pivot point

After three years, still driven to find career satisfaction, on the advice of a friend and colleague at the polytechnic, I made an appointment with a career counselor called Caroline Chu. The beginning was not auspicious. Her office was in Selegie House, a grey windowless building of small, cramped offices for professionals who could not afford the rents of the swish suites of Orchard Road.

Caroline Chu, on first appearance, did nothing to inspire my confidence. She was a slight, bespectacled lady with a dour expression. But I clung to the fact that she came highly recommended by my American friend Diane, who was in the same quandary as me. Armed with hope, Caroline and I started our one-hour consultation with a strengths-based assessment.

After what seemed like endless silence while she read my assessments, looking above her spectacles, she asked, "*Ah yah*, putting your career dreams on hold? Do you want to be in this position again?"

"Never again!" I replied emphatically, my throat constricting with unexpressed anger and frustration.

"But do you expect to be moving again, Yvonne?" She continued looking at me with a mix of intensity and curiosity in those deep-set black eyes.

"Yes, I'm afraid so," I said, sighing and averting my eyes to avoid her piercing stare. There was no point denying it. Graham was working on a fixed-term contract of four years. We had no idea where we would go next, just that we would be moving on again before long.

Without a good career reason to stay, Singapore was a 'no-go' zone and there was no way *my* career was going to magically become a reason for staying here. Frankly, it was a shambles. I stared out of the window at the dull concrete wall of the building next door, wondering if this was an omen of the future.

"Then we need to help you create a portable career!" Caroline said, reaching for her notebook. "We're going to start work right away. Owning your own business is the way to go since you have entrepreneurial strengths."

I took Caroline's advice to heart and left armed with the suggestions we had discussed. It was the best $100 I have ever spent in my life.

Caroline suggested I consider entrepreneurship, as I would then be in control of my career, rather than 'stopping and starting' with each relocation. This started me on a whole new trajectory of thinking about what my possibilities were. I couldn't wait to tell Graham what I had discovered that afternoon. It felt as if suddenly, through the clouds of frustration and angst, a golden key was being handed to me.

One humid late afternoon a few months later, Graham came home, his face aglow with sweat and excitement. He'd had a heart-to-heart conversation with the HR Manager that afternoon about the challenges that expatriates face when they arrive in Singapore. The polytechnic was going through a hiring spree of expatriate lecturers and she was wondering how to help the new hires settle down and integrate into life in Singapore.

"Here is the business opportunity you are looking for, Yvonne!" he said, his voice showing how thrilled he was for me. "You need to write a proposal and call Amy with your suggestion. After all, you are Singaporean and you have lived abroad, so you'll be able to help them."

It all sounded logical and simple enough. But where should I begin? It wouldn't be the first time I had started out not knowing much. But I knew I could always figure it out.

◎ **GOLDEN RULE #4: BE EQUALLY INVESTED IN EACH OTHER'S CAREER**

Applying the advice

Little did I know how pivotal this would be for the whole of my career. I quickly enlisted the help of my friend Anne, who was both an expatriate and family therapist. Together, we prepared a briefing folder and maps for each newcomer. We outlined an orientation program for new arrivals and inked the contract. I enlisted another friend, Mary, to cover for me when we had more than one family in town. We were off to a flying start and ready to welcome our first clients. Within the space of three months, I was off doing orientation tours with the newly arrived. I did most of the work, but, when I couldn't, Anne or Mary stood in for me.

In hindsight, this was the goose that laid the golden egg, and it would provide me with a career I love as we wound our way across four countries stretched over three continents.

Our next stop was the Philippines…

When we moved to the Philippines after Singapore, I took four years off to be with our young children, Antonia and Alastair. I relaunched my career when Alastair, the youngest, started pre-school. I started a small niche consulting company called Transitions Asia together with Filipino partners. Our focus was organizational development and cross-cultural training for companies with both expatriate and Filipino staff. The business grew until our clients included global companies, particularly in communications, manufacturing and banking. Soon we began doing orientation briefings for relocating staff and Accompanying Partners.

I have never looked back since that pivotal conversation with Caroline Chu that led to the start of my relocation business. Since then, I have been involved in the various aspects of managing globally mobile populations. And then, 22 years after that meeting with Caroline Chu, I landed at the World Bank, in charge of handling their globally mobile populations in Africa and Asia, which I did for nine years. Today, I work at the World Bank Group Family Network, which supports spouses and families of the World Bank Group employees worldwide. I continue to see the inordinately high price of global mobility on the career of the Accompanying Partner, which we will explore in the next chapters.

What does it take?

You may be wondering whether you and your partner have any hope of keeping both your careers alive despite international moves. The good news is that yes, you can, but it requires a genuine partnership, regular Dual Career Conversations and a commitment to use The CARE Code (which this book presents in later pages). It takes hard work and a partner who is as invested in your career as you are and vice versa. Then, and only then, can Dual Careers, in whatever form, work and thrive for both of you. You can be sure that a positive outcome is only possible if you create a way forward *together* and with *intention*.

Dual Career Conversations

Graham and I inadvertently stumbled on making these meaningful conversations a habit because of being bicultural. Right from the beginning we were forced to start thinking about what we wanted our relationship to be, where we could live – his country or mine – and more importantly, how to break the news to my mother that I was going out with a non-Chinese guy. (This was a big 'no-no' for her.) Decades later, we continue to have these conversations about our next steps and when and where we will finally go, and call 'home.'

◎ GOLDEN RULE #5: MAKE DUAL CAREER CONVERSATIONS A HABIT

Jennifer Petriglieri, Associate Professor of Organizational Behavior at INSEAD, draws from her research and extensive interviews with more than 100 couples hailing from 32 countries and ranging in age from 26 to 63. In her book, *Couples That Work*, she wrote, "Couples who thrived across their lifetime developed a habit of having conversations that go beyond the practicalities. [...] Busy couples often get understandably fixated on immediate issues – who cooks dinner, who picks up the kids, etc. But if it were as simple as dividing the housework and syncing our Google calendars, we wouldn't be talking today."

It is important to have Dual Career Conversations as a couple because often we make assumptions about each other, our non-negotiables, our hopes, our grandest dreams. Petriglieri believes that we leave issues like career privilege (whose career is considered more important) and coordination (how to coordinate two careers within our partnership) unexplored and unresolved and that we rarely voice our fears. Suddenly, life throws us a lemon and we resort to making hasty decisions based on practicalities and live to regret our choices (see Henry and Amelia, *Chapter 3, The Professional Follower*). Many an Accompanying Partner has told me that the impact of the decision to move abroad was underestimated.

Dual Career Conversations are not always comfortable, and they are rarely plain sailing, but they are imperative. If you have never done this before, it's never too late to start.

When we started out on our life journey together, neither of us knew what we really wanted to do. We knew there was the expectation that we would be successful. Being successful doing what? Graham went into teaching for lack of knowing what else he could do having graduated with a degree in Russian. In retrospect, it was all quite haphazard; we had no long-term plan except to be guided by circumstances.

However, thankfully we did some things right at the beginning. We were honest and open with each other, and we shared our career ups and downs. We were both supportive and committed to each other's success and we kept to our initial agreements of not being separated and not going to settle permanently in Singapore. Although I was not satisfied with my career at the beginning, I was tenacious in finding a solution, albeit not exactly quickly!

Over time and with experience, study and research, our approach to career planning evolved into what I now call The CARE Code. CARE is a mnemonic for the essential actions that Dual Career Couples need to take:

- **C**larify what's important to you individually.
- **A**ssess the challenges together.
- **R**efocus as needed.
- **E**xplore your options.

In this chapter, I have identified some Golden Rules and Common Pitfalls that Graham and I learned from our own experience. In *Chapter 2*, the stories of other Dual Career Couples indicate further Golden Rules and Common Pitfalls. In total, there are:

- 8 Golden Rules, which, if applied, help facilitate career coordination.
- 12 Common Pitfalls – mistakes we can inadvertently make.

While these Common Pitfalls and Golden Rules are powerful reminders of what can often occur, The CARE Code enables couples to go beyond merely avoiding such pitfalls and applying the rules. (You will find all the Golden Rules and Common Pitfalls gathered together at the end of the book in a handy *Quick Reference Guide*.)

Part Two provides exercises to address some of the dilemmas Dual Career Couples encounter. Hopefully, your individual responses and discussions as a couple will result in finding solutions to your challenges. These discussions lead to the co-creation of operating principles that will help you navigate the complexities of Dual Careers and international mobility. The CARE Code helps you work out your principles and priorities as a couple, including the non-negotiables. We worked ours out in the early years of our marriage, and this proved to be invaluable as we moved from one location to the next.

Points for Reflection

What resonated with you in this chapter?

Chapter 2

Dual Career Couples and International Relocation

In this chapter you will learn:

- How international mobility impacts the career of the Accompanying Partner.
- How to mitigate the risk when considering an international assignment.

I Didn't Want To, But...
Jo Parfitt, the Netherlands, 2020

I didn't want to move to Dubai after I got married but Ian, my fiancé, said that if I didn't, I'd "regret it for the rest of my life."

When, eventually, I relented, he promised me it would only be for "six months and then we'll see." He also promised that we'd take it in turns to have the lead career. So, he would start and then 'we'd see.'

To join Ian, back then, in 1987, meant that I had to close down my business. My successful business. A partnership with my father, also a writer and trainer, and another trainer. It cost me £1,500 to leave Windmill Word Processing Services. I gave Ian the bill.

In one fell swoop, by agreeing to join Ian in Dubai, I left my country, my family, my friends and the flat I had just purchased. I left my professional identity and my 'own money,' said "I do," and jumped on a plane.

I resented Ian for forcing me into this and it took me 10 years to forgive him. Ten whole years. I know it seems like I am repeating myself here, but believe me, I was a broken record. And yes, we did have those Dual Career Conversations. Every time we sat down to discuss what we would do either because Ian had a career opportunity, or I had another idea for my own business, we'd agree it was 'my turn' but then we'd look at the bottom line – the money, the perks – and recognize that I could never match what he could earn; and so, in full but reluctant agreement, I'd back down again. So sure, we had the conversations and sure, we both agreed with the outcome, but inside, a piece of my self-esteem chipped off every time.

But then, after a decade and back in the UK after living in Dubai, Oman and Norway, I realized that I had been lucky. I had been in a better position than Ian. I had been able to make choices, follow my dreams, take risks, change direction, learn, explore and do fulfilling, often lucrative, freelance work that left me as much time off as I needed. I could be there for our children and our visitors. I could take long summer vacations. Meanwhile, Ian had few choices. He was stuck with a 9 to 5 job that required many more hours than that, golden-handcuffed to a career he usually liked well enough but rarely loved. I had the privilege of being able to do what I loved. And now I'm glad. So glad. My career, complete with its twists and turns, has made me into the published author of over 30 books, a publisher, a mentor, a teacher and, still, at my core, a writer. I even wrote the first book on the portable career, called *A Career in Your Suitcase*. Oh, the irony!

I hadn't wanted to be so difficult, unreasonable and ungrateful but I was. I'm a woman with a degree and a professional identity that is like a second skin. I closed my business in 1987 and it felt like I'd said goodbye to who I was forever. I was wrong. If I wish for anything to be different it would not be that I had insisted on taking my turn, but that I had reframed my thinking earlier and not given my husband such a hard time. I wish I'd appreciated my good fortune from the start.

I didn't want to, but... is a typical dilemma faced by Dual Career Couples. It occurs because often the discussion on career prioritization does not take place at the outset. As in Jo and Ian's story, the initial agreement is 'six months and then we'll see.'

These words marked the trajectory of Jo and Ian's journey as a Dual Career Couple. What made Jo close her thriving business to join Ian in Dubai? Could he not have found a job back in the UK instead? Jo left her life behind without a plan. How were they going to make this work? 'Whose career' was left unexplored and an assumption was made that one partner would follow the other.

Often our assumptions are based on gender, cultural and generational stereotypes. What would happen after six months? This remained unanswered at the point of decision. What does 'we'll see' mean for Ian's career and Jo's career? Perhaps if this had been clarified at the beginning, Jo would have been able to have her turn and not end up backing down because, "I could never match what he could earn." Although they both agreed with the outcome, the price was "a piece of my self-esteem chipped off every time." The story of Jo and Ian is typical of many Dual Career Couples because we often make decisions based on what is expedient and/or practical. A better approach would be to also discuss how a globally mobile life can accommodate two careers and how we can manage this as a couple.

Jo's frustration was the consequence of her reluctantly agreeing not to take her turn: "I resented Ian for forcing me into this and it took me 10 years to forgive him." It was only resolved when Jo was able to reframe her thinking and see that she was lucky to be able to follow her dreams. Once she understood that, she began to thrive. Seven moves on, she has a thriving publishing and authors' mentoring business that is not dependent on location.

Many Accompanying Partners never reach the point of being able to reframe the situation, find new ways of using their skills or reinventing their careers and beginning to thrive. They limp from assignment to assignment steeped in victimhood and seething with anger and frustration. Very few hit the ground running and arrive with job in hand. Why do so few Accompanying Partners thrive?

The Conundrum That Won't Go Away: Career Prioritization and the Dual Career Couple

It is generally accepted in both research and business that a Dual Career Couple is defined as a couple where both partners have a commitment to their professional careers and their relationship, as described by van Gils & Kraaykamp in a research paper in *International Sociology* in 2008.

Dual Career Couples are not only highly committed to their careers, but they also have expectations of future advancement. Both are generally well educated, due to assortative mating (the tendency for people with similar levels of education to marry one another). This has increased by 25% over the past three decades. Career prioritization is an issue that most Dual Career Couples face anyway, with or without relocation, because their career aspirations, as well as the commitment to being together, produce a tension over whose career takes precedence. Yours, mine or ours?

It becomes more complicated when one partner is offered a career opportunity that requires an international relocation. International assignments are a career accelerant. In many global companies, an international assignment is considered a prerequisite for an executive/senior leadership role. Many studies also show that professionals benefit from a geographic move because of increased knowledge, networks and economic gains. Research from the Center for Global Development shows that knowledge workers who take international assignments earn higher salaries when compared with those who perform the same tasks in the same jobs at the same firms at the home location. Thus, the opportunity for an international assignment cannot be easily surrendered.

The Expat Lab barometer results for 2019 show that "64% of expats consider expatriation to be positive on their careers and 57% have improved their standard of living. After returning home, 58% still think that the impact on their careers has been positive." But this positive impact of international mobility on career is experienced often by *one* partner only; the career privilege rests only with one of the two. So, what becomes of the career of the other, especially as, according to the 2018 Relocating Partner Survey Report, 77% of partners are working prior to the international assignment?

Assuming the family unit or couple want to be in the same geographical location, the other partner will likely have to give up their job. It can be hard to avoid a situation where the career ambitions of one partner are put into storage once the decision has been made to accompany the other partner. This happened with Jo and the consequences gnawed away at her for many years.

The challenge that these couples face is career prioritization. How do they make this work? Generally speaking, the most common approach to solving this dilemma is for one partner to take what is euphemistically called 'a career pause' to accompany the other. I did so for Graham and Jo did it for Ian, as you have read.

The 2018 Relocating Partner Survey Report shows that 71% of employees who are internationally mobile are male, 29% are female. In another survey, conducted by Expat Communication in

2019, of 3,000 French expats, 33% of Accompanying Partners reported that they had sacrificed their careers to 'follow' their other half. One can only assume, given the number of male mobile employees, that the career sacrifice is largely borne by the female Accompanying Partner.

As just mentioned, 77% of Accompanying Partners work prior to relocation. Moreover, this situation is not about to change, because the percentage of working partners is sharply increasing with each generation. While 67% of baby boomer partners are professionally active, this grows to 86% with Gen X partners, and to 90% of Gen Y partners, who will soon become the majority of mobile employees. Given the increasing numbers, the problem will become exacerbated.

A Punishing Landscape for the Partner

The relocation landscape is punishing for the Accompanying Partner as the temporary career pause can have a significant emotional impact. As reflected in the Expat Insider 2019 survey results, 57% of Accompanying Partners are not working while on an international assignment. Much of our identity is tied up with our careers, which provides us with our sense of purpose. The culture we come from also affects how we feel when our professional identity is lost.

A workshop participant was in tears as she recalled her breakfast conversation that morning. "Amy, our seven-year-old daughter, looked up from her cereal bowl and asked quizzically, 'Mummy, Daddy goes to work, I go to school, what do you do?'" This innocent comment opened the flood gates of raw emotions – grief, loss and anger – that flow so easily in unguarded moments. She continues, "Even my child has a role. Everyone does, except me." And this is how 'pieces of self-esteem are chipped off.'

It should therefore come as no surprise that, according to the EY/ NetExpat 2018 Relocating Partner Survey, approximately 70% of professionals cite partner unwillingness to move because of career as the main reason for not accepting an international assignment. Likewise, 71% of companies report that an unhappy, unintegrated partner at the host location is the main cause of assignment failure.

Why is this the case? What are the problems that escalate for couples when on an international assignment? At one of my workshops on career management for the globally mobile professional, I asked the question: "How many of you expect to be moving again?" Every hand was raised. We went on to discuss: "What is difficult about being a globally mobile professional and an Accompanying Partner?" I received a variety of answers, including:

- "Having to start again."
- "Challenging but need to fight on."
- "You need to be a fighter."
- "It's hard taking on the caretaker role suddenly as it doesn't fit the vision you had."
- "The feeling of a sudden stop."

When their partner had accepted the international assignment, they had not fully understood the implications of the move for them as the Accompanying Partner. This is because such a move opens up a range of uncomfortable issues that go beyond the mere practicalities of packing up and settling down in a new location. These issues, include:

- Social norms
- Parenthood
- The expatriate lifestyle

- Hidden losses, such as identity, financial independence and support network
- Lack of career opportunities
- Lack of a work permit
- Lack of language ability

For each issue, detailed discussion is required, with agreements being reached. Without discussion and negotiation, frustration, resentment and anger are inevitable. In addition, an unhappy partner may find it harder to settle in. Some may, like Jo, feel disappointed for many years.

Enter the Great Disruptors

Social norms

Perhaps the greatest culprit is the assumptions on which we base our decisions. For example, cultural norms in most countries are still strongly rooted in the notion of the male breadwinner. I was raised to believe that when push comes to shove, it is my husband's career that takes precedence. Yet I come from a 'progressive' family that prides itself in educating the women in the family. In 1918 my grandmother was one of the first Asian women to attend university in the USA.

Until and unless we confront those assumptions, our default position will be what we were raised to believe. Shani Orgad, author of the book *Heading Home*, interviewed highly-educated professional women who left their jobs after having children. She writes, "The decision was as much about facilitating their husband's continued career advancement as it was about their desire to spend more time with their children." From her interviews, she also discovered that, "However, often indirectly, with pain and pause, many of them admitted that they have unwittingly deferred their identities to their husbands. When the two-earner household could not cope with the pressures of both partners combining paid work and parenting, it was the woman who gave up her job." And it would seem to be the same in the majority of cases when it comes to international relocation.

Parenthood

Parenthood is a disruptor in the life of any couple. Often, couples rely on extended family support to navigate the challenges of childcare, school vacations and work-related travel. The proximity of social and practical support is removed when a family relocates. Settling into school, setting up home, etc., generally falls into the lap of the Accompanying Partner, even in the most egalitarian of relationships. For example, the long school holidays coupled with the need to visit family is often incompatible with local employment leave allocation. Moreover, women generally start to focus on their own job search only after the children have settled down in their new location. Young adult children at university still need support and increasingly these days, for the sandwich generation, eldercare is an added complexity.

That said, for the younger Dual Career Couples, an assignment is seen as an opportunity to have a child since the relocation will already be a career disruptor for the Accompanying Partner.

The expatriate lifestyle

Sometimes the realities of daily life make it hard. One partner describes her life thus: "My husband has to work more than 80 hours a week just to accomplish his tasks and he travels 60% of his time. With young kids, work for me is prohibited. Then, changing jobs or having a career on my side is impossible at the rate of rotations."

The length of contract and the frequency of rotations (involving a move to a new location) impact the ability of the Accompanying Partner to continue their career. The length of assignment for most public and private sector organizations is three to four years. This is how a partner of an international civil servant describes her life: "Each time we move, I have to resign from my place of employment and then it takes time to find something in the new location and, by the time I have settled into a new job, we move again and I have to resign again. It means that we have to make a choice about which spouse's career to prioritize." Clearly up to now she has had the short straw. Her story is typical, as the statistics reflect, and one of the top frustrations of Accompanying Partners is the 'stop-start' syndrome, which leads to resentment, marital stress and loss of employability.

On the brighter side of things, one overseas assignment, if strategically planned, can be the 'lift-off' pad for the career of the Accompanying Partner. This works well for mid-career professionals. Maggie was one such person. She was a teacher in the Netherlands and took leave of absence to accompany her partner on a three-year assignment to the USA. She decided to use that time to take a career break and learn a new skill to add to her career assets. She spent time working with a start-up and then went on to study UX design. She has returned to a higher-level position within the education system as an 'experienced designer and educator.'

If career prioritization is not explicitly discussed, the cumulative effect of multiple rotations will impact the career prospects of the Accompanying Partner. Resentment may build up, which may also stifle the ability to identify opportunities.

Hidden losses, such as identity, financial independence and support network

In all likelihood, the Accompanying Partner has a strong professional identity, financial independence and a sense of purpose. Yet, in the twinkling of an eye she becomes John's partner, Olivia's mother; she becomes invisible. This results in a potent mix of hidden losses. Hidden losses are not visible to others and sometimes even to oneself for a time because they can be camouflaged amidst the good. For example, often relocation offers the opportunity to have household help, time with children without having to juggle a hectic work/travel schedule, and travel to exotic locations. Types of hidden losses include loss of relationships, dreams, status and identity. According to Dr Robert Neimeyer, Director of the Portland Institute for Loss and Transition, "We're capable of losing places, projects, possessions, professions and protections, all of which we may be powerfully attached to." This causes grief.

In order to move on we need to lament and then replace our losses. In Jo's case, it was reframing her situation and understanding that she was lucky because she had the luxury of following her dreams and the good fortune to do what she loved. For me, it was knowing that I had put in place a solution so it would never happen to me again. This meant developing a strong skill set and expertise in managing mobile populations. In the Philippines, it was forming a consultancy with Filipino partners. When we moved to the USA, I decided to use my skills in-house within the World Bank Group. Otherwise, there is a very real possibility of spiraling into an abyss of anger, resentment and frustration.

Lamenting our losses, coming to terms with regret and finding the emotional capacity to rebuild a new identity takes time. If you find this overwhelming, it may be helpful to work with a transition career coach or seek professional help.

Doruk, a Gen X engineer from Turkey, perceptively described his experience as a 'systems crash' and as having to do the hard work of living through the grief cycle. The late Dr Elisabeth Kübler-Ross developed a framework for us to process our grief over the losses that we experience in life. Loss, and the grief that ensues, could arise just as well from the loss of a support network as from the end of a relationship or the loss of a partner or job. The grief cycle, as shown in the diagram below, is not necessarily experienced sequentially, nor does everyone come to acceptance.

Kübler-Ross Grief Cycle

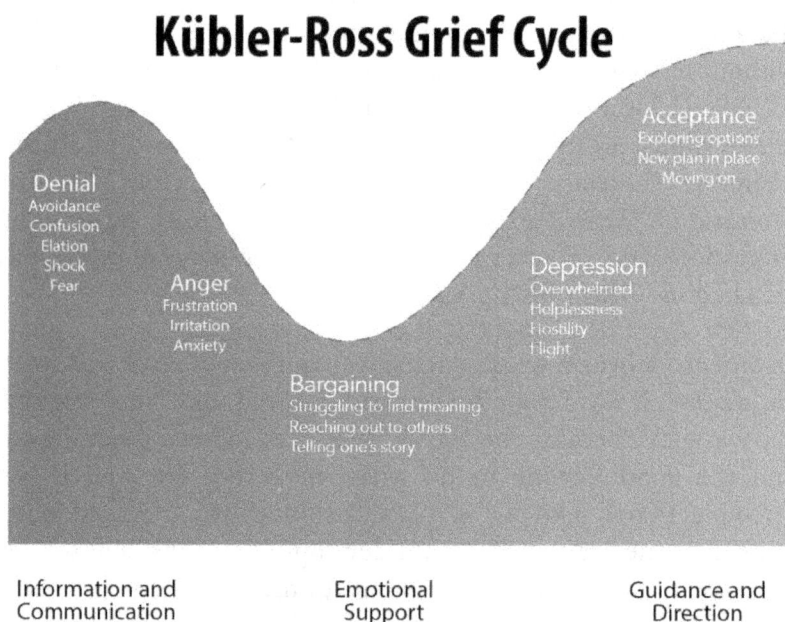

Acceptance
Exploring options
New plan in place
Moving on

Denial
Avoidance
Confusion
Elation
Shock
Fear

Anger
Frustration
Irritation
Anxiety

Depression
Overwhelmed
Helplessness
Hostility
Flight

Bargaining
Struggling to find meaning
Reaching out to others
Telling one's story

| Information and Communication | Emotional Support | Guidance and Direction |

Kübler-Ross Grief Cycle (psycom.net)

Processing grief and loss can take time. Doruk took three years to get up and running again, to re-establish his professional identity. Although he was a graduate of a top university at home, he decided to take a certification in project management to gain recognition for his competencies in a new country. It seems that for most, even when the decision is taken jointly, it still results in a roller-coaster ride of ups and downs, gains and losses.

Lack of career opportunities

Certain career skills are more transferable than others. For example, professions such as medicine, psychology and law often require recertification and/or licensing, depending on the country, in order to practice. On the other hand, skills like software development, data analytics and graphic design are more transferable.

Depending on location, often the local employment market does not offer the Accompanying Partner comparable career opportunities. This, combined with the stage of the Accompanying Partner's career, can make finding a comparable position in the new location extremely challenging. At this point, many Accompanying Partners resort to accepting the job at hand. Often, they not only have deviated from their careers but also find themselves underemployed in the job they have accepted. Hence it should not come as a surprise that 33% of expatriate partners claimed that they sacrificed their careers to follow their partners, according to the Global Survey 2017 by Expat Communication.

Lack of a work permit

The 2012 International Mobility and Dual Career Survey of International Employers undertaken by the Permits Foundation found that 51% of employees were unlikely to relocate to a country where it is difficult for a partner to get a work permit.

Work permits for Accompanying Partners are not always easily attainable. According to the Permits Foundation, there are currently 35 countries that allow the (married) partner or sometimes even the accompanying (unmarried) partner or children to work freely. The issue of obtaining a work permit is even more complicated for same-sex partners as countries vary in their acceptance of non-traditional partnerships or marriages.

In fact, only 20 countries recognize same-sex marriage. This is no blueprint for making the world your oyster.

Even when a partner can secure a work permit, local employment laws may restrict what jobs are available to foreigners and employment protocols may 'put off' local employers from hiring foreign staff. The hurdles are many and nuanced. National employment laws and regulations change frequently in some countries, often at short notice. If you want to work while on assignment, it is vital that you check with your partner's employer that this is possible. The Permits Foundation provides an evolving list of countries that have favorable work permit regulations for the Accompanying Partner. Ensure that you have the most up-to-date information prior to making your decision as the situation is very fluid. For example, many countries took a more protective stance with work permits for foreign nationals as a result of Covid-19. Also, check what the process to acquire the work permit involves. Although costly, it may be better to employ a local immigration lawyer to handle your application. This ensures a higher rate of success, especially in countries that require navigating bureaucracy.

Often, work permit restrictions are more flexible when it comes to entrepreneurship and small business owners. Entrepreneurship is often seen as a means of creating employment for nationals, whereas employment is seen as taking a job away from its citizens. Covid-19 and technology have opened many more opportunities for remote work, which facilitates career continuity with the same employer, although restrictive national laws can make this more challenging. Nevertheless, it is an option to explore.

Overall, work permit restrictions remain one of the main barriers to career continuation for even some of the most motivated, determined and proactive Accompanying Partners.

Sylvie's story

Where there is a will, there's a way as far as Sylvie was concerned. Her husband was assigned to Mozambique and although she could speak the language (Portuguese), partners were not allowed to work; in fact, they could not even volunteer. Sylvie wanted very much to work, and she was not going to be put off so easily. She discovered there were jobs she could apply for, but she needed to find a way around the restrictions. Fortunately, she found one. "I learned that if I formed my own company and became an investor, I would be able to work. It was not easy. I had to use an HR company to help get all the paperwork done. I also had to return to my home country to apply for the correct visa. And when we leave, I will not get back the money I invested. Getting a work permit is costly and the bureaucracy is immense, but I want to work so I am prepared to do the hard work to make it happen."

Lack of language ability

What if you do not speak the language of the country of assignment? It is one thing to be able to go to the supermarket and hail a cab. It is a completely different ball game to be able to function in a foreign language in a professional environment. In some countries, speaking the local language fluently is obligatory if you are to find employment.

What makes it so challenging for the Accompanying Partner to come to terms with the new landscape is the cumulative effect of all these variables, coupled with the need to redefine their identity and rebuild their self-confidence. But these disruptors can be mitigated.

Mitigating the Disruptors

When it comes to career continuation and coordination, *where*, *when* and *for how long* you go can be pivotal in determining whether you can operate as a Dual Career Couple. Remote work offers Dual Career Couples a greater range of options. The simplest and most obvious solution would be to ask your employer if you could work remotely or transfer to the local organization if your company has a presence there. However, rarely does life work out in such neat, tidy packages. This means that you will have to consider how best to mitigate the challenges, given your own circumstances.

Nevertheless, there are certain aspects of a move that can minimize disruption, including:

- Timing of the assignment
- Location of the assignment
- Duration of the assignment

Timing of the assignment

When is the right time to accept an international assignment? This is a question that is deeply personal to each person and couple. These are the main considerations:

A. **Lifecycle**: Is this life stage conducive to a relocation for you and your family? For example, many couples choose to relocate when they want to start a family, or when the children are young. For some, this is seen as a short career break to raise a family and therefore work permit considerations are not important. Others choose to relocate to countries where household help is more affordable and available. Others wait until they are empty nesters to embark on a new adventure. Generally speaking, families try not to relocate during the high-school years or they try to ensure that the length of the assignment covers the high-school years and the location has a good international school.

B. **Career cycle**: Where are you in your career? Is your partner's career at a point where it can tolerate a degree of disruption? For example, we accepted our first international assignment so that Graham would gain international experience to strengthen his linguistic credentials. Laurent, another accompanying spouse, on the other hand, agreed to move with his partner to the USA after practicing medicine for about eight years so that he could get a master's degree in public health. The qualification would enhance his medical credentials and enable him to have a greater impact as a physician or as a public health specialist.

Location of the assignment

Location can be a disruptor but proper planning, research about employment opportunities and intentional communication between the couple can mitigate the disruption to the career of the Accompanying Partner. When we meet Anjana in *Chapter 3, The Professional Follower*, we will discover that she had moved to Armenia where she couldn't work, and so she studied international development instead. This was then followed by a move to Brazil where she could work but couldn't speak the language. The cumulative effect of these two moves resulted in reams of frustration and anger, plus an employment gap of at least six years by the end of their assignment in Brazil.

The following three snippets illustrate how you can mitigate the location disruptor.

Julia's story
If you want to work, then choosing to go to a location that enables you to work has to be a priority. I vividly recollect Julia, a staff member, coming to me, desperate that I help find her partner, Steven, a job in Hong Kong. Steven was a US-trained cardiologist whose one non-negotiable was that he be able to continue in his

profession; otherwise, the move was off. Julia was completely desperate, as if fighting for her life, when she came to seek my help. Julia had just been offered her dream job in the Hong Kong office and did not want to miss the opportunity.

She was fortunate on three counts:

1. The position was based in Hong Kong, which allows married partners to work.

2. He was prepared not to practice medicine, so long as he could work within the profession.

3. I had lived and worked in Hong Kong and had personal experience of the working world there.

We discussed a few options. I suggested that teaching at a university might be something for Steven to consider. This is quite a common career pivot for doctors who do not wish to spend years doing 'residency' again to get their license to practice in the new location. Julia spent her next few business trips to Hong Kong working very hard on her husband's behalf. There is a happy ending to this story. Indeed, he secured a position at a teaching hospital in Hong Kong and the family relocated there. In this case, a 'win for one' was experienced as a 'win for all.' And the icing on the cake was live-in household help to look after the twins.

⊙ **GOLDEN RULE #6: THOROUGHLY RESEARCH EMPLOYMENT OPPORTUNITIES IN THE NEW LOCATION BEFORE YOU GO**

Rada's story
Rada had already had a four-year employment gap because of having her daughter and being based in South Africa where partners could not work. Upon relocating back to Washington DC, she started working toward re-entering the workforce. At the same time, conversations between her husband and his boss were

taking place about a possible move, with Delhi and Vienna mooted as possible options. When they discussed the choice of location, she refused to go to Delhi, as this would short-circuit her career again, but agreed that Vienna was a viable option because she could work there. Employment opportunities were good and it was not too far from Bulgaria, which was home for her. However, her husband was not selected for the position based in Vienna. He was offered Delhi instead, but he refused the position. They remained in Washington and she now has a job and is happily re-established professionally.

Sophie's story

I was impressed that Sophie, an architect by training, was able to pursue her career in Sydney and Amsterdam. Now that she was back in the USA, she was going back to her teaching position at the local university. "How did you do this?" I asked excitedly because I knew that this was quite a coup. Clearly and without hesitation she replied, "I refuse to move until I have a job offer in hand, and this time we agreed that I needed to resume my career at the university, so we came back."

Duration of the assignment

Discussing the duration of the assignment is critical to the ability of the Accompanying Partner to continue his or her career. It should fit into your long-term career plan. Generally speaking, it is possible to manage a career break for two to three years without making too much of a dent in your resume. However, make sure that you are doing something to enhance your employability during that time. Others take a break to raise a family, study to increase employability or do a career pivot. If you intend to work, then assignments of three to four years are a better option. It gives you time to find a position and contribute to the organization. Two-year assignments are better suited for secondments or leave of absence. Furthermore, seasoned expatriates would know that it generally takes at least six months to settle into your new location, not to mention the time needed to obtain a work permit and carry out a job search. A two-year assignment would hardly give you any time to establish yourself in the job. Ensure that any break does not morph into an employment gap and suddenly you become a candidate for re-entry into the workforce.

◎ GOLDEN RULE #7: AGREE ON THE PARAMETERS FOR POSSIBLE ASSIGNMENTS

Given the combination of factors, is it any surprise that partners are reluctant to move because of the impact on their career? As I said before, one of the main causes of assignment failure is the inability of the Accompanying Partner and/or family to adjust to the new location. One Accompanying Partner describes herself as, "Struggling with the change of roles from professional to stay-at-home mum, from financial independence to complete dependence on a single income." A single income that is not even hers! The adjustment chasm is immense.

As we conclude the discussion on mitigating the disruptors, we need to stress the importance of a Dual Career Conversation about *when*, *where* and *how long* an appropriate assignment would be for you and your family. This will provide you with a roadmap that can guide your Dual Career Conversations, career aspirations and decisions, as well as help you to build a more flexible skill set to enable you to have more career options. This may include learning a foreign language ahead of time so that you will be able to achieve a level of confidence and fluency. Computer programming is another skill that is portable and possible to continue remotely. Unlike client-facing roles, it is more forgiving if you can't speak the language of business at your location. If you want to work, there is no substitute for doing thorough research on local employment opportunities and the dynamics of the local market for your particular skill set.

Points for Reflection

What resonated with you in this chapter?

Chapter 3

The Professional Follower

In this chapter you will learn:

- The consequences of not thinking about and discussing career prioritization.

- The Common Pitfalls to avoid so as not to become a disgruntled Accompanying Partner.

- The challenges of being a globally mobile professional and Accompanying Partner.

A typical demographic profile of an Accompanying Partner across private and public sector organizations shows that the partner has at least a bachelor's degree. More than 50% have master's degrees and worked prior to international relocation and, more importantly, want to continue working while globally mobile. We have seen in the previous chapter that it isn't easy to find comparable career opportunities abroad for the Accompanying Partner. Many 'follow' at great personal cost to their careers.

The Accompanying Partner Syndrome

"I loved my job, but I had to leave to follow my husband."
"I underestimated the cost of moving with him."
"I am tired of having to stop and start with every relocation."
"We discussed it, but I didn't think she would get the job."

These are typical comments I hear today in my work as a Dual Career specialist and no different from the thoughts that milled round my own mind for many years too. Graham and I did not really talk about what international relocation meant for us. Since being separated was a 'no-go' zone for us, it meant one accompanying the other, regardless of the opportunity cost. At the outset, Graham's career path was clearer than mine, so he called the tune. In fact, there was nothing to keep me on my own track as I was drifting anyway.

If you recall, I slipped into the role of Accompanying Partner inadvertently. On reflection, decades later, I realized I let go because I lacked clarity about my own career goals and was unaware of what was possible.

Partner career support has always been close to my heart, and it has been my professional focus since 2007. The faces of my clients flash through my mind when I reflect back over my years as a Dual Career specialist – Amelia, Anjana, Maria, Silvia, Yusof. It is their stories that leave an indelible mark on me because, for a time, their stories were my story too.

COMMON PITFALL #5: YOU READILY AGREE TO FOLLOW BECAUSE YOU ARE CURRENTLY NOT VESTED IN YOUR OWN CAREER.

All these people are well-educated professionals in their own right, with careers of their own, until, one day, by design or coincidence, their partner is offered a job that involves an international move. Some are Accompanying Partners by choice, but more often than not, one career progresses at the expense of the other. Others have drifted into it or been caught unawares, ignorant of the implications of their decision. Just like it happened to me.

Regardless of which camp you fall into, the problems may vary, but solutions are only found with intent. It's complicated because the impact of the decision that one career takes precedence over another lives on years after the boxes have been unpacked for the umpteenth time. This book attempts to unravel this complexity.

What the Partners Say

The Accompanying Partner

Meet Amelia
Amelia and Henry are both British and were happily living in London, where Henry worked for a consulting firm. Amelia, an interior designer, had a full client load and was busy and fulfilled by her projects.

One warm summer evening we were sipping a glass of wine in the garden of a mutual friend in New York. Once she found out that I was a Dual Career specialist, Amelia's story flowed faster than she could drink her wine and suddenly she was no longer in the garden but reliving the nightmare of how they made their decision to move.

"I did not have a career; rather I had a very unusual and unusually well-paid part-time job which I loved," said Amelia, looking wistful as if savoring the fading memories of the perfect occupation. She continued, incredulous with hindsight, "Our decision to move was made when we had a one-month-old baby, a toddler of two, and Henry was working 12 to 16 hours a day. There was certainly no opportunity to talk at any length in between sleepless nights, entertaining an active toddler and Henry's work." Two months later, the family found themselves in New York. Amelia was blind-sided.

"The shocking isolation that comes when you arrive in a city where you have never lived, know no one, can't work, and can't work out the cultural points of social connection," is how, looking back, she describes this devastating experience.

Then the weeks became months, and the months became years.

"The growing frustration turns into anger and then bitterness when you realize your work as you knew it will never be there again," she continued. "You have totally de-skilled, you have no possibility of meaningful work on the horizon, and you have no idea how to reconstruct your intellectual or work life in a foreign country, or even potentially in your home country anymore! From there, it's very hard not to dissolve into depression and anxiety."

In the case of Amelia and Henry, the emotional cost of the decision to move was underestimated. Nor should a decision like this be made in a hurry or when one or both partners are experiencing emotional and/or cognitive overload. Something as important as this cannot be rushed in the hope that by some stroke of good fortune things are going to work themselves out.

COMMON PITFALL #6: YOU DON'T TAKE SUFFICIENT TIME TO THINK ABOUT THE IMPLICATIONS OF THE MOVE FOR YOU

Meet Anjana

Both Anjana and Aryan are from India. When Aryan was posted to Armenia for three years, Anjana knew she couldn't work there because of work permit and language restrictions, so she decided to use this time to get her master's in organizational development. Armed with a newly minted degree, Anjana accompanied Aryan to his next posting in Brazil. She did not speak Portuguese, however, making it impossible to get a job using her new qualification. Here, language was a major hurdle.

One day, I received a telephone call from Anjana. She was desperate.

I was immediately struck by the depth of her increasing disappointment and frustration at her inability to continue her career. Her voice crackled with emotion.

"How did I end up in the same predicament twice in a row?" she said. "There wasn't much of a conversation with Aryan about where we should go next; after all, he should know I want to work. Didn't I just invest three years studying?" She was painfully aware that if she didn't get to work while they were in Brazil, she would have an employment gap of six years.

This outcome is typical of what happens when a couple do not take the time to communicate openly and honestly. Decisions are based on incorrect assumptions and a lack of long-term planning. The couple would have done well to discuss where might be the best place for both of their careers.

With Anjana, the decisions were piecemeal. For example, the decision to study while she was unable to work was a good one. But insufficient thought was given to career coordination and continuation with her partner when it came to next steps.

COMMON PITFALL #7: YOU DON'T DISCUSS YOUR CAREER CONTINUITY AND COORDINATION, WHICH LEADS TO ONE PARTNER HAVING TO 'STOP AND START' WITH EACH MOVE

Meet Camilla

Aatos and Camilla are both from Finland. I met Camilla because she was part of my research on how Dual Career Couples make career decisions.

She describes how they decided to come to Washington DC: "I clearly remember when he told me that he was selected. He had been applying for months for various positions and quite frankly had given up hope of hearing back from the organization. I was very happy and proud of him and could tell it was important for him although I had never heard of the international organization, except once in my history class when I was 10. We did not really talk about what it meant for us. In fact, we did not have 'the' talk; he simply asked me if I would come. I said yes right away."

Camilla is not the only partner I've met who has told me this. Camilla sums up her own situation in a way that will resonate with many. "We were both young and very naive. When you are offered a job like that you have to react fast. Maybe we should have talked about him applying to those jobs in the first place, but we did not."

COMMON PITFALL #8: YOU DON'T FIND OUT ENOUGH INFORMATION ABOUT YOUR PARTNER'S PLANNED MOVE

Meet Hao

Hao is from Vietnam, Jaspar from Canada. They met while working in Hanoi. Hao's career as a management consultant was flourishing and successful; Jaspar worked for a US global consumer goods company. When her husband had to return to the USA, Hao thought long and hard about what this would mean for her career. By this time, they also had a baby and she thought it would be better for them as a family to be together. I will never forget her comment during one of the workshops I facilitated when she said, "I underestimated the cost of moving with him." Her voice was hardly above a whisper, but her pain was palpable.

COMMON PITFALL #9: YOU UNDERESTIMATE THE COST

Meet Matteo

Matteo is from Italy, Arlene from Croatia. They were based in Brazil where Matteo was a plant manager for a global manufacturing company and Arlene worked in public health. She was then offered an opportunity in Washington DC. They had visited Washington while based in Brazil as Arlene's sister worked there, and they liked the city very much. They decided to accept the offer and move to DC to be closer to family and live in a city they wanted to discover. However, Matteo found it difficult to find a job as his expertise in manufacturing did not translate well into the local job market. He would have been much better off in the Midwest. But work permit regulations did not allow him to work outside the Metro Washington DC area.

Matteo is one of numerous partners who believe they will 'find a job.' But reality is harsh. He and many others like him are finding it hard to land a job.

COMMON PITFALL #10: YOU DON'T GET INFORMATION ABOUT THE LOCAL EMPLOYMENT MARKET IN RELATION TO YOUR SKILLS

The male Accompanying Partner

You may have noticed that in most of the examples thus far, the Accompanying Partner is the woman.

Research by the Clayman Institute for Gender Research at Stanford in 2008 showed that among those respondents who earn more than their academic partners, 61% of men and 44 % of women consider their own careers more important than those of their partners, whereas 37% of men and 51% of women consider the careers of both partners to be of equal importance. In other words, higher-earning men in academic couples assign greater importance to their own careers, whereas higher-earning women more often assign equal value to both careers. In the decade since the study took place not much has changed. Indeed, the 2018 Relocating Partner Survey, conducted by NetExpat in conjunction with EY, showed that 71% of mobile employees are male and 78% of Accompanying Partners are female.

In my work, I often get calls from female staff about what programs we offer to support the male Accompanying Partners. I have yet to have a call from a male member of staff about what programs we have to support his partner! The only request I have ever had from a male member of staff was to ask if I could help him by telling his partner about their impending move!

Maybe it is true after all, that men are from Mars and women from Venus. John Gray, author of the book *Men Are from Mars, Women Are from Venus*, highlights the key differences between men and women in how they think, act and communicate. A criticism that is often leveled at John Gray is that the differences between men and women are not scientifically proven; while there may exist broad differences between men and women, these are culturally and not biologically produced. Although there may be some truth in this, many of his observations are broadly accurate.

When it comes to making work a priority, men have the weight of culture and tradition behind them to propel them to make work and being the 'provider' their priority. This is not to say that men do not care about their families but, when push comes to shove, work/career becomes the first priority. The numbers also tell the story; as I said, 71% of internationally mobile employees are male.

In 2014, Robin Ely and her colleagues conducted a survey of 25,000 Harvard Business School MBA graduates. The survey states that "more than half the men in Generation X and the Baby Boom said that when they left HBS, they expected that their careers would take priority over their spouses' or partners'." Some may argue that this is a generational difference. However, the findings of this survey also show that "half of millennial men expect their careers to take precedence over their partners'. Only a quarter of millennial women expect their partners' careers to take precedence." Moreover, "Two-thirds of millennial men expect their partners to take primary responsibility for raising children."

Perhaps personal expectations of career, family and societal norms make it more difficult for male partners to change their attitude.

This shift in gender roles has put partners in a vulnerable position, as they struggle with feelings of powerlessness, despair and isolation. For others, this drastic role reversal in their relationship is not something that had been anticipated when they decided to accompany their partners. During my interviews with male Accompanying Partners, I discovered how deeply ingrained gender norms are even in males raised in more egalitarian cultures. It becomes even more challenging when it is outside of their cultural norms.

Dr Nina Cole of Ryerson University, in her article on expatriate Accompanying Partners, notes that when men assume trailing partner status, their sense of identity is often negatively affected by not successfully fulfilling the role of breadwinner for their family. Forret, Sullivan, and Mainiero, in their research on gender role differences, contend that a perceived loss of masculine and professional identity can lead to feelings of defeat among men, where changes in gender roles, as well as a lack of understanding from others relating to the unusual status of a female breadwinner family, may create barriers to undertaking international assignments.

The stories of most male Accompanying Partners that I have met in the course of my work certainly support the academic research.

Meet Azizi

Azizi, another of my workshop attendees, comes from Tanzania. He recollects how his friends back home reacted when he told them he had agreed to follow his wife on a posting to Washington DC. "They asked me if I was going to become the chauffeur now that my career was taking a back seat." Three years on, he is still asked how much longer he plans on being a househusband by his incredulous friends. He is an entrepreneur and financially independent. This acts as a buffer to the snide comments and caustic jokes of his friends. Otherwise, it is a big dent in one's ego and self-esteem. Other male partners have mentioned how these types of comments erode their self-confidence.

Meet Aslan

Aslan is a mid-career oil executive. During one of my workshops, he graphically describes how he is feeling: "I feel like a hunter locked in a cage but all the usual keys don't work, so I can't get out." He continues, "Now I find that I have to make my own keys." This captures the essence of the challenge of being a male Accompanying Partner. Other male Accompanying Partners have shared the despair and loneliness of not being able to express how they truly feel. Sadly, some have admitted to not even being able to share with their partners their feelings of isolation, their fears of not being employable, loneliness, and so on.

COMMON PITFALL #11: YOU DON'T FULLY UNDERSTAND THE UNINTENDED CONSEQUENCES OF ROLE REVERSAL

Meet Jawara

Jawara, a Nigerian lawyer, describes his decision to accompany his wife as a "team decision" and says that he had to "put aside cultural norms." He concludes, "Most of my friends and family think I'm crazy and 90% of males would not do what I have done. In our culture, I am described as 'a man with no bones.'" During our interview, he stressed the importance of having a team vision and clarity of purpose: "Otherwise, you don't stand a chance."

Both research and anecdotal evidence show that the ability to adjust to being a male Accompanying Partner is a complex combination of individual factors, culture and gender.

What Are the Issues?

During one of my workshops, I divided the male and female participants into separate groups to discuss the difficulties of being a globally mobile professional and Accompanying Partner.

They found there were many similar challenges, but the main difference was that the male Accompanying Partners felt 'just not prepared' for the change in role. Firstly, most were raised with a traditional mindset about the male being the breadwinner and his career taking precedence over that of his partner. Those who come from more traditional cultures feel this more acutely and many talked about the disappointment they have become to their families for accompanying their partners. Many have pointed out that this is especially challenging when your parents don't understand your actions. They report that parents often ask, "How can you be following your wife?" They also shared how ill-prepared they were for domestic chores and becoming the main caregiver to their children. However, they also acknowledged that as a result of being the main caregiver they have a much closer relationship with their children.

Difficulties of being a globally mobile professional and Accompanying Partner

Female	Male
Loss of financial independence	Lack of recognition of prior employment experience and university degrees in certain destination countries
Loss of support systems, including childcare support from extended family	Loss of financial independence
Being asked, "What do you do?"	Sacrifices (especially career) made to follow partner
Loss of career ('not just a housewife')	Career on hold, a challenging decision
Women taking an unequal share of work and childcare	Change of role
Lack of recognition of prior employment experience and university degrees in certain destination countries	Need to learn new skills, e.g. cooking, childcare
Navigating a new cultural environment	Ill-prepared for role reversal, have to be taught
	Navigating a new cultural environment

Source: Career Lab workshop, input from participants, 2019

Male and female Accompanying Partners face both similar and unique challenges due to both culture and gender. The most challenging difference for the male Accompanying Partner is the expectation of their own role and how others see them. Many male

Accompanying Partners have experienced a lack of acceptance by their own peers.

What Happens to Accompanying Partners on International Assignments?

Industry surveys, such as the 2019 Brookfield Global Relocation Trends Survey, the 2019 Internations Business Solutions Survey and the 2018 Relocating Partner Survey by NetExpat and EY put numbers and percentages to the names and stories of the Accompanying Partner. It does not make for happy reading.

An increasing number of companies expect highfliers to get some overseas experience. According to Brookfield, 27% of global companies indicated that international work experience is a prerequisite to being part of a global leadership team. The Relocating Partner Survey showed that a massive 77% of Accompanying Partners were working prior to assignment and, once they arrive, 66% report to be looking for work. On the other hand, the Internations Business Solutions Survey of 2019 reported that only 25% were working full-time and 18% part-time.

In addition, the statistics hide a high degree of underemployment as, anecdotally, many expatriate partners report taking jobs that are well below their capabilities simply because it is the only way for them to work. Just like what happened for me. In fact, a 2016 survey published by Expatriate Communication showed that 62% of expat partners reported that expatriation is 'negative' or 'very negative' for their careers.

It is clear, therefore, that international assignments adversely affect the careers of Accompanying Partners because they find it extremely difficult to find work appropriate to their level of expertise and/or they are ill-prepared for the challenges ahead.

According to the 2018 Relocating Partner Survey, 97% of mobile employees actively involve their partners in the discussion prior to accepting an assignment, and partners concur they are usually significantly involved in the decision-making process. And yet, stories like those of Amelia, Anjana and Camilla are more the norm than the exception. Why does this happen?

It is fairly common that decisions are not given much thought and are largely based on practicalities, in the moment choices and financial gain, to name a few. But what has been overlooked is that most mobile employees are part of a Dual Career partnership. According to van Gils and Kraaykamp in their article for *International Sociology* in 2008, Dual Career Couples are defined by a commitment to professional careers in combination with a commitment to the relationship by both partners. Furthermore, companies offer the job to an individual, and their partner is left to redefine their career (though some companies do offer spousal support). Whichever way you turn, the picture is not rosy for the Dual Career Couple.

Dual Career Couples are aware of this: 70% of males and 79% of females cite 'partner unwilling to move because of career' as the main reason for refusing an international assignment. Conversely, both the Permits Foundations Survey of 2009 and the 2018 Relocating Partner Survey still cite that the main reason (71%) for assignment failure is an unhappy, unintegrated partner at the host location. It isn't rosy, because it is a complex problem, and it requires attention and intention on the part of both the individuals and organizations for this to work.

Dr Yvonne McNulty writes in her research paper for *Human Resource Development International* (2012), "Scholars have found that powerlessness, loss of identity and changes in dynamics with partners contribute to trailing partners' feelings of isolation, frustration, disappointment and anger during international assignments." Interviews with partners found that self-doubt and lack of confidence is a resisting force for otherwise well-educated, career driven partners. Many of the partners indicated that fear of change, low risk tolerance and uncertainty were factors that played into their self-doubt and loss of confidence. Therefore, if international assignments are to succeed, support is needed to help Accompanying Partners redefine their identity and find meaningful work.

Are You Following Along?

Do you recognize aspects of yourself in any of the stories in this chapter?

The assumption has to be examined that, if we cannot accommodate two careers within the context of our relationship, then one career has to be sacrificed at the altar of family good. For most well-educated partners, the internal drivers, like the sense of achievement and the desire to make a difference and to be recognized, cannot simply be snuffed out because your partner's career has taken precedence. Yet you have assumed the follower role.

Isabella poignantly recalls, "We were working for the same organization, and I gave up my job to give career priority to my partner who was actually at a lower grade than I was at the point of my resignation. I did it so we could move as a family." This was a conscious career choice.

Gender does play a role in career prioritization strategies and decisions. Research by Marja Känsälä et al. (2014) demonstrated that the female expatriates in their study had a more flexible approach to their careers, and/or were more willing to prioritize their partner's career and to refuse other job offers for the benefit of the relationship. Male partners tended to take a more hierarchical approach. Unfortunately, as one partner so aptly said,

"I think the whole system and process is designed for one partner to be 'trailing.'" Sadly, I think evidence proves her right.

> **COMMON PITFALL #12: YOU ASSUME THAT YOUR ROLE IS TO FOLLOW AND THAT YOUR CAREER IS AUTOMATICALLY THE SECONDARY ONE**

Fortunately, change is possible. It can begin with you. Women, in particular, should challenge the assumption that their role is to follow or that their career is automatically the secondary one. In the end, we need to look beyond the practical details, compensation packages and career privilege of one partner that comes at an inordinate cost to the other.

You may, after discussion with your partner, decide that his/her career should take precedence for now. But this has to be a shared decision.

Furthermore, don't be afraid to renegotiate your career continuation strategies at different junctures of life. Boris Groysberg and Robin Abrahams, in their article 'Marriage and the Marketplace: Dual-Career Couples in the 21st Century,' show that, for Dual Careers to work, a 'win for one' must be experienced as a 'win for all.' They go on to say that "if it is experienced as a 'win' for the individual executive at the expense of the needs of the marriage or the family, disharmony will result."

> **GOLDEN RULE #8: A WIN FOR ONE MUST BE EXPERIENCED AS A WIN FOR ALL**

Can We Create a Win for All?

A study by Marja Känsälä et al. also shows international assignments strengthen traditional gender roles amongst male expatriates. The statistics below support their findings:

Impact of international mobility on the career of the Accompanying Partner

- 79% of Accompanying Partners work prior to international assignment of partner.
- 65% of Accompanying Partners are not working during the international assignment.
- 78% of Accompanying Partners are female.
- Nearly 80% of women and 70% of men cite partner unwillingness to move because of career as the main reason for not accepting an international assignment.
- 33% of Accompanying Partners reported that they 'sacrificed' their careers to follow their partners.

It paints a rather gloomy picture of international assignments for both couples and employers. For Dual Career Couples, international mobility and career prioritization is clearly a multifaceted challenge because career goals and a commitment to each other and the family are equally important. This creates a tension that can get out of hand unless careful consideration is given to the question: Whose career will it be – yours, mine or ours?

The Case Studies in *Chapter 4: A Win for All* show how six couples have tackled the challenges of international relocations in relation to their careers. Although they made mistakes along the way, they have largely been successful in achieving their goals. 'Success' entails both partners experiencing the international assignment as 'a win for all.' 'The winner takes it all' approach generally ends unhappily for all.

✎ Points for Reflection

What resonated with you in this chapter?

Chapter 4

A Win for All: The Career Stories of Six Couples

> In this chapter you will learn:
>
> - How six Dual Career Couples managed their careers in relation to frequent international assignments.
> - Models and strategies couples can adopt.

Both globalization and dual income couples, of which Dual Career Couples are a subset, are on the increase throughout the world. Even in countries like Japan, where numbers have been historically lower, they are now on the rise. Managing two careers across borders increases both the complexity and the challenges for both partners. No two couples are alike, but certain strategies for career continuation and coordination work better than others. In this chapter we will be looking at the stories of six Dual Career Couples and how they managed both careers worldwide over time.

What they have in common is that they are all Dual Career families. According to Dr Linda Duxbury, Canada's most accomplished researcher, writer and speaker on work-life balance, a Dual Career family is defined thus: "Both partners have a high level of education and income, both have career goals of their own and derive a 'psychic income' as well as a financial one. Their careers are important to them."

These Case Studies are true stories. They cover the challenges and the actions taken to move their careers forward. However, the Dual Career families in these Case Studies have chosen different strategies to navigate their chosen paths of realization. While the six strategies are outlined below, it is important to note that no couple needs to be wedded to a single approach; given the twists and turns of life, flexibility may often be required. However, central to the success of all these couples is their ability to communicate with each other while being mutually supportive. As you read the Case Studies, you will notice the key actions taken by the couples to influence 'our' careers. These actions form the basis of the Keys to Success, which are listed at the end of each Case Study.

Case Study 1: Turn-Taking – Robert and Rosemary

Turn-taking is a strategy where the couple decide who should claim the career privilege when making a career decision for a particular job opportunity, while the other agrees to make the sacrifice this time. One partner may have the privilege twice in succession depending on a raft of factors, which include the stage in his/her career, their family situation and the opportunity being presented. It is understood and accepted by both partners that the career privilege changes hands.

Case Study 2: Double Primary – Melissa and Christian

The double primary strategy has the career goals of the couple as the key driver. Often, the couple will decide on a long-distance or commuter arrangement (i.e., weekends spent together if geography permits) to ensure that they are both able to pursue their careers. In this arrangement, couples are willing to take more risks and make sacrifices for their career. This focus on career does not negate their commitment to their relationship.

Case Study 3: Primary-Secondary – Maja and Henrik

This follows the traditional pattern of the male being the main breadwinner. All career decisions are therefore driven by his career trajectory and the partner accompanies him and tries to find employment as and when she can. The assumption that the woman has to 'follow' is rarely challenged by either the man or the woman. This primary-secondary model also results in the Accompanying Partner experiencing 'stop and start' fatigue as she has to move on with her partner and leave a job and friends. Not surprisingly, this can lead to a level of resentment toward the lead partner for having the sole career privilege.

Case Study 4: Role Reversal – Amanda and Simon

In this arrangement, traditional gender roles are reversed. This creates challenges for the male Accompanying Partner as it breaks with culture, social norms and expectations. It also creates new realities to navigate. According to Duxbury: "The women in this partnership have a very high level of career commitment and also receive a high level of 'psychic reward' from their jobs. This family type is likely to prove challenging for both partners, as it requires having to navigate a very powerful and robust system of traditional societal norms and renegotiate roles within the family, and the balance of power is highly correlated to each partner's access to resources, i.e., paid employment."

Case Study 5: Combination of Turn-Taking, Primary-Secondary and Role Reversal – Cielo and Charles

This approach is often typical of a millennial couple who usually begin coupledom as double primary and, as the relationship evolves, so does the career model. They make the change to accommodate career ambitions and international mobility. Generally, couples have a more egalitarian mindset and have a more fluid career model to accommodate life goals too.

Case Study 6: Non-Traditional, Same-Sex Couple – Chuck and Chen

This arrangement is often very similar to role reversal families in that the traditional gender roles are shattered. In many ways, couples come unfettered to write their own script, but they also face huge cultural and societal barriers. Many countries still do not accept same-sex couples as a family entity, so they encounter immigration restrictions. The options where they can live and work across the globe are limited, creating additional career challenges.

Case Study 1:
Turn-Taking – Robert and Rosemary

Overview

After eight international moves over 16 years and two children, Robert and Rosemary are still traveling the world as a Dual Career Couple. Both have been able to work wherever they have lived, but they had to accept that their approach of *taking turns* in terms of whose career took priority would affect their career progression. Nevertheless, they can look back and say that they made the right decision. "Neither of us has progressed as far as we would have, had we either stayed in Australia or only focused on one career, and that gets frustrating at times. All in all, life has been enriched more by going than by staying," says Rosemary.

Their Dual Career Journey

The Problem: Robert is Australian and Rosemary is from New Zealand. They meet as students in Australia in 1996 over their shared love for mountaineering. Upon graduation in 1999, Robert gets a job with the Australian Government. In 2001, armed with a PhD, Rosemary accepts a position with a software start-up company in the USA and this marks the beginning of their long-distance relationship. By 2003, they realize that a long-distance relationship is not much fun and not something they want to continue doing.

> Agreed not to settle for a long-distance relationship.

The Response: After considerable discussion and much research, Robert takes leave without pay (LWOP) to join Rosemary in the USA. Working visas for unmarried couples are virtually impossible to get. But true love is not easily deterred so Robert goes to the US on a J-1 visa, which offers cultural and exchange opportunities in the US. He begins 'work' as a research assistant at a university near Rosemary. He recalls that he was underemployed. He had always been driven by the compelling vision to study, so he enrolls in a distance learning course (postgraduate fees in the US are very high). As Robert explains,

Searched for options. Studying was one of them.

Agreed on the key principle.

"We are both from different countries, so having to decide where to go next was very much a feature of our relationship from the beginning, and we also agreed not to make decisions that would hurt each other's careers."

Consequently, in 2004, when Rosemary is offered a job in Dunedin, New Zealand, they accept, as Robert can work there without a work permit. It isn't quite the job of Rosemary's dreams, but it offers Robert the opportunity to work. So he decides to resign from the Australian Government.

Willing to accept second best for the good of one's partner.

Fortuitously, Robert's boss refuses to accept his resignation and extends his LWOP till December 2005. What they don't anticipate is the type of work opportunities that Dunedin will offer Robert. "Yes, I could work but again I was underemployed," says Robert recalling their time in Dunedin. (As discussed in *Chapter 2, Dual Career Couples and International Relocation*, research shows that underemployment is one of the major career challenges encountered by Dual Career Couples on international assignments.)

Reviewed the current situation and considered options.

Decision-time once again: It is now December 2005, and Robert has come to the end of his LWOP and has to return to Australia if he wants to resume his employment with the Australian Government. They also know from lived experience that good career opportunities are limited in Dunedin. They decide that Robert will return to his position with the Australian Government as this would give him job satisfaction and a clear career path. This time, Rosemary accompanies Robert back to Canberra where she starts to look for a job in the private sector.

Took turns.

Robert starts back at the Australian Government as an international security analyst. In April 2007, they make a conscious, intentional decision for Rosemary to leave the private sector to join another Australian government agency. This means a pay cut. You may be wondering, w*hy did they do that?* They did so because the public sector offered greater flexibility and generous leave options.

Planned ahead.

Uprooted again: In 2008, Robert is posted to Hawaii for two years. Where does that leave Rosemary, who is enjoying her new job? Avoiding a long-distance relationship is key for the couple. Rosemary therefore gets permission to work remotely. However, they also decide that this is an ideal time to start a family. Rosemary is able to 'continue employment' using a combination of remote work, maternity leave and LWOP options to see them through the duration of Robert's assignment. Robert is quick to point out that none of this happened just by chance. Tough decisions like a pay cut were taken earlier on, in return for flexibility and leave options later.

Made the most of life's trigger points.

Planned ahead.

Next steps: When they return from Hawaii, Robert assumes another internationally-focused position. Rosemary returns to work with her agency on a part-time basis as they have one child and are planning on having another. Robert also starts to target a posting at the Australian Embassy in Jakarta.

He is successful and in 2012 the family leaves for Jakarta for a four-year posting. Rosemary is on paid maternity leave followed by LWOP. They have two young children and household help. Life is almost idyllic until in mid-2014 Rosemary is made redundant. This is how Robert recollects this time in their lives: "We decided to invest her redundancy pay-out in career focused retraining. She eventually decided to do a distance learning course run by the University of Leeds in the UK on geographic information systems (GIS)."

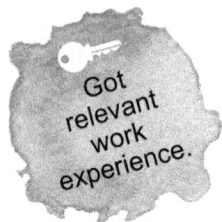

Made the most of adversity.

Through networking channels at their child's pre-school, she hears about a volunteer opportunity at a UN agency that is automating its GIS analysis processes. What begins as a volunteer position morphs into a paid consultancy.

Got relevant work experience.

Networked.

Home again: They return to Australia at the end of 2016 and Robert takes up a US-focused position with the Australian Government. Rosemary continues working as a consultant for the UN but travels a lot to Indonesia and Sri Lanka. Soon her remit of countries increases, and she is traveling for about one-third of the year; Robert's job also entails a lot of travel and they are grateful for the grandparents who help out with the children. Rosemary is also getting restless and tells Robert that she would like another overseas posting.

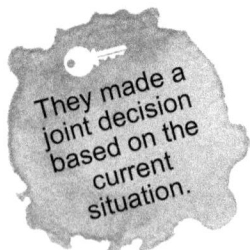

They communicated their concerns to each other.

Taking turns once more: One day in 2018, when Rosemary is in Munich and Robert is in Washington DC, she is offered a job at an international organization, which is coincidentally based in Washington DC.

They made a joint decision based on the current situation.

Robert describes this as an easy decision as they are both frazzled with travel and, in his words, "We had forgotten what the children looked like."

This time Robert takes long service leave from his work, and the family relocates to DC in the summer of 2018. Robert uses his long service leave to rethink what he wants to do with his career. He is now working for a boutique risk consulting company. As he says, "Soon we will hit the halfway mark in Rosemary's contract, and we will start discussing what we want to do next. Do we renew the contract? Where do we want the children to go to high school and university?" These are the questions they will work out together.

Discussions never stop.

What can we learn from Robert and Rosemary's story?

◎ **GOLDEN RULE #3: SET YOUR 'NO-GO' AREAS EARLY ON**

They established two basic no-go areas – one for their personal lives and one for their careers:

1. Avoid a long-distance relationship.
2. Never make decisions that would hurt the other's career.

◎ **GOLDEN RULE #2: MAKE SHARED DECISIONS**

1. All decisions to move were shared, and career decisions affecting each of their careers were discussed.

⊚ GOLDEN RULE #5: MAKE DUAL CAREER
CONVERSATIONS A HABIT

1. They use life's triggers and checkpoints and plan ahead.
2. They look for opportunities.

Keys to Success

1. Turn-taking to be the principal job holder. This means Robert's career took priority for their move to Indonesia and Rosemary's to Washington DC.
2. Joined an organization with a global bandwidth to accommodate movement.
3. Strategically used company benefits, employment policies and leave options to ensure that the Accompanying Partner would have continued employment in some form and so would not have a gap in their resume.
4. Returned to base. After each overseas assignment, returning to base allows the Accompanying Partner to recalibrate their career. In this case, it is Australia where both had equal career opportunities unhindered by work permit and/or language restrictions.
5. The partner whose career was not being prioritized used the time to reskill, upskill.
6. Made conscious career choices. For example: targeted assignment, pay cut to join the public sector, invested redundancy money to add another skill set.
7. Peppered with good fortune – supportive bosses along the way, working for the Australian government.

Case Study 2:
Double Primary – Melissa and Christian

Overview

After 17 years, Melissa, Christian and their children are still on the move. Throughout their relationship, both of them have been very invested in their careers. As a result, they adopt the *double primary* strategy, where the career goals of both of them are a key driver in their decision-making. This is especially the case early in their careers, when they are apart for the best part of six years. They take risks, moving on average every two years. This includes moving five times to be together or to move closer to each other. Melissa sums up the past 17 years by saying, "We both know that our careers are equally important, independently from the directions they may take. This means we also take risks. Being apart hasn't been easy, but we have both found satisfaction in our work and our careers have flourished."

Their Dual Career Journey

The Problem: Melissa, who is French, and Christian, who is German, meet in Sarajevo, Bosnia, in 2003. She is working for the French NGO Handicap International as a project manager, and he is a consultant for the World Bank. In early 2005, Christian has to return to Washington DC, where the World Bank's headquarters is located. But, not being American, Melissa will not be able to work without a US long-term visa. Meanwhile, Melissa is offered a position as a Junior Professional Officer (JPO) by the French Ministry of Foreign Affairs in Afghanistan.

The Response: They discuss the problem and agree that their individual careers take priority in their lives. However, their relationship is also very important, and so they explore ways in which they can somehow combine the two. This included choosing destinations that were a plane ride away and had good connectivity so they could communicate daily.

Melissa turns down the JPO offer and is offered another job with an NGO based in Brussels. She explains the situation to her new employer (now The International Campaign to Ban Landmines) and suggests working remotely from Washington DC. Amazingly, the employer agrees. But like Christian, she is traveling a lot and so starts thinking about the next step. "Working remotely suited me as a temporary arrangement, but I needed a job where I could fully invest myself," says Melissa.

Discussed the problem and agreed on the principle to follow in determining the way forward. Agreed on prerequisites to maintain their long-distance relationship

Looked for job opportunities and negotiated working arrangements.

Decision-time twice over: In 2006, Christian is offered a staff position at the World Bank, but it means being posted to Bulgaria. He can't turn this career opportunity down. Melissa decides to join him and continues working remotely in Bulgaria, but after four months, she is offered a job in New York with the United Nations Development Programme (UNDP). "This was the job I had been waiting for," says Melissa. "There were not many humanitarian work opportunities for me in Bulgaria, and so, difficult as it was to have a long-distance relationship, moving to New York was the only viable option. We agreed that once we had both moved up the career ladder, we would have greater flexibility with regard to future job choices."

Career came first, for Christian…

… and for Melissa.

Decided together in line with their principle.

On the move again: The two years they spend living on different continents aren't easy, even though the jobs are fulfilling. However, in 2008, Christian returns to Washington DC, which is not too far from New York. For a year, Christian commutes to NYC nearly every weekend. But Melissa then accepts a new assignment in the UNDP's office in Cambodia in early 2009. "We found this decision very difficult to make but kept to our principle of prioritizing our careers." At the end of 2009, they get married.

Made another decision, based on their principle.

The best years: In early 2010, Christian applies for a DC based position working on Vietnam and a few months later is able to relocate to Vietnam. For two years, he is based in Vietnam and Melissa in Cambodia. They meet every other weekend somewhere in Southeast Asia. "These weekends allowed traveling to multiple exciting places in Southeast Asia and we have fond memories," says Melissa. In 2012, Melissa joins him in Vietnam, and they decide to start a family while she takes up some distance learning.

Recognized the importance of living closer to each other and spending time together.

Made the most of new opportunities, e.g., studied.

Turning down a job offer: "After nearly four years in Vietnam, it was time for him to move on, and I was also ready for a change from Southeast Asia," says Melissa. Christian is asked to apply for a position in the Ankara, Turkey, office. They discuss this at length and decide not to go because: 1) After 10 years abroad, Melissa is ready to move somewhere where she can easily blend in; and 2) There is

Established a clear rationale for their decision.

Constant communication.

no obvious career opportunity for her, aside from looking for short consultancies. After nearly two years of being home-based (studying, consultancies, looking after the baby), Melissa says, "I was ready to fully invest myself in a new endeavor." Their

Supported each other by listening and advising, keeping their basic principle in mind.

rationale for not going to Ankara is the result of their good communication. "We have career conversations very regularly, almost daily every time there is an opportunity, or when we are thinking about our next move," remarks Melissa.

Made plans to explore new opportunities.

Onwards to Brussels: Christian is then offered a job in Brussels, which is ideal for them as a family. A few months later, and while pregnant with a second child, Melissa accepts a job as Chief Operating Officer for Blue Square, a tech/data company. When Christian's four-year contract comes to an

Career remained a non-negotiable priority.

end, he manages to negotiate an extension for another two years as Melissa is not willing to move on from Blue Square and they want to give the family further stability. They stay there until 2019, when they return to Washington DC.

Back to Washington DC: This is how Melissa describes their decision to return to DC: "In 2019, DC was a good move for the two of us. It allowed Christian, after 10 years abroad (four in Vietnam and six in Brussels), to reconnect with HQ." Melissa by this time is ready for a mid-career reinvention and wants to explore transitioning to a new or different career. Also, Blue Square is interested in setting up

Remained on the lookout for career opportunities for both of them.

an office in DC to be closer to the US market and so she agrees with the CEO that she will continue to work part-time for them. This gives her time to explore her options.

They are now happily living in DC. While they will give it a few years for Melissa to explore options and give the children some stability (and time to learn English), they look forward to exposing their careers and their kids to some new environments in the future.

What can we learn from Melissa and Christian's story?

GOLDEN RULE #2: MAKE SHARED DECISIONS

Their shared decisions include:

1. Living and working in different locations from each other.
2. Refusing the job in Turkey.
3. Requesting an extension in Brussels.
4. Agreeing to return to Washington DC.

GOLDEN RULE #5: MAKE DUAL CAREER CONVERSATIONS A HABIT

1. They have Dual Career Conversations very regularly, every time there is an opportunity, or when thinking about their next move. Almost daily if a move is being considered.

⊙ **GOLDEN RULE #4: BE EQUALLY INVESTED IN EACH OTHER'S CAREER**

1. They are each other's best advisor.
2. They share their thoughts, doubts, aspirations all the time. They listen to each other and support each other in any way they can.

⊙ **GOLDEN RULE #8: A WIN FOR ONE MUST BE EXPERIENCED AS A WIN FOR ALL**

1. They both at times did not pursue opportunities that would have stopped them being closer after many years apart or would have made it difficult for one of them to find work.

Keys to Success

1. Both knew and appreciated how much their careers mattered to them.
2. Both were willing to take necessary risks.
3. Maintained clarity about priorities – made the decision early on in the relationship that career was a priority for both of them, even if this meant being separated. But also chose their destinations based on connectivity, i.e., able to communicate on a daily basis and where possible be a plane ride away from each other.
4. Put in the hard work of maintaining a long-distance relationship.
5. Leveraged the organization's global reach to target career opportunities and managed their careers to get nearer to each other when separated. For example, Melissa worked remotely when Christian was in DC in 2005, and Christian moved to Hanoi (Vietnam) to be closer to Melissa in Cambodia.
6. After starting a family, only moved to locations where both partners could work.
7. They benefited from supportive managers who enabled the move to Vietnam and the extension in Brussels. Christian in turn had to demonstrate his value and show how they would benefit from him being at the respective locations.

Case Study 3:
Primary-Secondary – Maja and Henrik

Overview

After university, Maja and Henrik both embark on successful careers, but in different countries. They get married a few years later and live and work in Stockholm. But Henrik works for the Swedish Ministry for Foreign Affairs and so overseas postings are going to be a regular feature of their married life, which will likely affect Maja's career. Realizing that one career may need to be prioritized, they agree on how best to accommodate the other's career. Over the years, this has led to some frustration, but with careful management, planning ahead and clear communication, they have managed to overcome the challenges.

Their Dual Career Journey

The Problem: When Henrik and Maja, who are both Swedish, meet at university, they are both focused on their future careers. Upon graduation in 1993, Henrik joins the Swedish Ministry for Foreign Affairs and Maja takes a job with a management consulting company. But two years later, Maja is transferred to the company's office in Brussels. Fortunately, this is only for a year, and upon returning to Stockholm, she switches companies yet remains in the private sector. After they marry in 1997, Henrik is posted to Japan. Obviously, she is aware that marrying a diplomat will eventually lead to this situation, but how will this affect her career? How can they manage this situation?

The Response: Before they got married, they discussed what they would do were this situation to arise. They don't want a long-distance relationship, and both understand that Henrik's job is going to involve postings to different locations every few years. "We agree that Henrik will only accept postings to locations where I will be allowed to work," says Maja. "Also, we will alternate between an overseas posting and time in Stockholm. This will enable me to continue with my career." She also deliberately puts herself forward for timebound or phased projects so that staying two to three years will not have an impact on her employment prospects or her employer.

Discussed the problem and agreed on the principles:

• No long-distance relationship.
• Henrik's career was the primary one.
• Accommodated Maja's career by refusing postings where she can't work and alternating between overseas and Stockholm.

Adopted a plan to increase job mobility.

To increase job opportunities and/or transfers, Maja finds a job with a Swedish global company in Japan. This is a wise decision, as she is able to continue working for the global company on their return to Sweden, thus minimizing the disruption to her career. While in Japan, she also finds the time to learn Japanese, recognizing that you should never turn down an opportunity to learn a new skill or language.

Followed their principle

Worked and developed new skills (learned Japanese).

Planned ahead.

Preparing for the next overseas posting: In 1999, they return to Stockholm, where they both resume their old jobs. However, knowing that the next overseas posting for Henrik will soon come, Maja does her research and finds that the public sector gives generous leave of absence, thus providing job security for when she returns home. It also enables her to look for other job opportunities when abroad. As a result, in 2002 she leaves the private sector and joins the Swedish civil service. The downside of this choice is that the Swedish civil service does not have global offices. But on balance this is a good decision as it provides job security for when she returns.

On the move again: Sure enough, the next posting for Henrik comes just a year later, in 2003. This time it's Canberra, Australia. As planned, Maja takes leave of absence and spends the three years in Australia working on various consulting projects. She also takes the opportunity to start a family.

Didn't follow their principle. Had valid reasons, but it affected her career.

Next stop, in 2006, is Vienna, Austria. This time, they go directly from Canberra to Vienna, without returning to Stockholm. Maja admits, "I know this was contrary to our basic principle of returning home between postings." She agrees to this because, "It was a good job opportunity and career move for Henrik. He has family in Austria and we both spent some time studying and living in Vienna as students. It was not an unfamiliar country to us and felt close to home. I knew that I would get an extended leave of absence."

In the early months in Vienna, Maja tries hard to find a job. In fact, she is interviewed by a UN agency. During the interview, she realizes that being a diplomat's wife and not having parents to rely on for childcare is seen as a liability in Austria. She adds, "It is a very conservative culture and many parents rely on

Made the best of the situation when she couldn't work.

grandparents to help out. I decided to enjoy the time with my children and to study German and law to make good use of my time."

Accepted that she had primary responsibility for looking after the children.

In 2009, she has a second child. She says, "If we had lived in Sweden when we had our children, the situation would have been different. We would have shared the responsibility more equally."

Maja's acceptance of her career as the secondary one: How does Maja cope with her career being put on hold, given her determination to have a career? At the outset of their relationship, a successful career is a priority for them both. However, after a series of consecutive moves and an extensive career gap, Maja realizes that, so long as Henrik works for the Swedish Ministry for Foreign Affairs, they will be following the primary-secondary career model. She has made strenuous efforts to maintain a career but acknowledges that hers is secondary to her husband's. Yet Maja's positive outlook recognizes the reward from living in new and different countries and the opportunities that this offers.

> Recognized that her career will always be secondary to Henrik's.

> Had an explorer's mindset, which enabled a positive outlook.

"I am curious about the world and about different cultures. I want to experience and learn new things. Going on a posting is a great opportunity. It's an explorer's mindset. I have always felt it's a choice I have made. No one has forced me into anything," she says.

Several years at home: They return to Stockholm in 2011. Maja has been on leave of absence for eight years. She has new skills she would like to use in process development to improve efficiency and effectiveness. She researches her options and leverages her network and lands a new job in another Swedish agency. But she remains within the Swedish public sector.

> Back home, Maja worked again to keep her career going.

The next five years in Sweden allow Maja to consolidate her career before it is time for another posting. Does she ever tire of this 'stop and start' with her career? This is how she describes it: "If you want to work, you have to think ahead. I have done research into work opportunities and work authorization and discussed it with Henrik before he applied to any postings. We have always discussed his applications for postings and agreed that he would not apply for postings we're not both willing to accept. Since we had our children and as I got older, job security, together with making sure I can get a leave of absence from my employer in Sweden, has been very important to me as well." She continues, "Finding a new job with each posting is not an easy task. It's a challenge and sometimes I have failed. When I have been able to get a job, the rewards in terms of personal development and learning are great. This is what motivates me. I'm not afraid of failure. If I fail to get a job, I find other ways to keep developing my skills and do something meaningful with my time."

Always discussed possible postings based on research into work opportunities for Maja.

Found other opportunities to develop skills if no job opportunity. Not afraid of failure to find a job.

Overseas once more: In 2016, Henrik gets posted to London. Maja uses flexible work policies to continue working for the first year. She decides to use the remainder of her time in London doing an online qualification in Leadership and Organizational Theory to enhance her skill set while also raising two children. After two years, Henrik goes to Washington DC to take up a representational role for the Swedish government. Maja is still

Studied again and raised the children.

Still on the lookout for job opportunities.

on leave of absence and applies for work authorization in the US, which takes several months to obtain. And then Covid-19 hits.

What can we learn from Maja and Henrik's story?

⊙ **GOLDEN RULE #2: MAKE SHARED DECISIONS**

1. They discuss which posting Henrik will apply for before he submits his application.
2. They agree jointly on which posting they are both willing to accept.

⊙ **GOLDEN RULE #3: SET YOUR 'NO-GO' AREAS EARLY ON**

1. They agree at the beginning of their married life that Henrik will only accept postings to locations where Maja will be allowed to work in some capacity.
2. They don't want a long-distance relationship, and both understand that Henrik's job is going to involve postings to different locations every few years.
3. They agree to try, as far as possible, to alternate an overseas posting with a home posting so that Maja can resume her career.

⊚ **GOLDEN RULE #5: MAKE DUAL CAREER CONVERSATIONS A HABIT**

1. They have Dual Career Conversations each time one of them is about to make any sort of change in their careers and if one of them feels a need to have a discussion. They have change-initiated discussions every second or third year and always before applying for new postings or new jobs.
2. They discuss their careers frequently, probably once or twice each month, but it really varies a lot with what is happening at that point in their lives.

⊚ **GOLDEN RULE #8: A WIN FOR ONE MUST BE EXPERIENCED AS A WIN FOR ALL**

1. Their co-ownership of the decision to accept each assignment was a crucial factor in Maja not feeling that she was forced to go.
2. The decision to go to Austria was a deviation from their plan to return to Sweden after each overseas assignment. But the promotion, together with having family in Austria, enjoying time with the children and being closer to home, made this a win for all.
3. Maja makes the most of each posting. She looks for opportunities to expand her skill set and adopts an explorer's mindset about living in different countries and cultures.

Keys to Success

1. They make joint decisions about which assignment to apply for. This includes doing research about the countries they are considering: what are the work permit restrictions and job opportunities for each location?
2. They are clear about their priorities. Henrik only applies for positions where Maja can work, and they alternate between an overseas posting and Sweden so she can return to work.
3. Maja is intentional about the companies she works for; for example, she works for a Swedish global company that has offices abroad and in Sweden.
4. Maja deliberately switches from the private sector to the public sector because of generous leave of absence policies, which are protected by law. This offers job security when posted back to Sweden and the possibility of switching to different government agencies. She was on leave of absence from 2003 to 2011 and is so again from September 2017 until the end of their assignment in Washington DC in 2022. It also means a quick re-entry into her last position when they return to Sweden.
5. Maja knew that as a diplomat's partner she would have to move frequently. She also knew that she wanted to work, so she developed her own strategy. This meant having clarity about who she is, her current situation and where she would like to be in the future.
6. Having the right mindset has been equally important for her success. This is what she calls "an explorer's mindset," being curious, open-minded and unafraid of failure.
7. Maja has not worked while on every assignment; sometimes she has done a combination of consultancies and studies to enhance her skill set or has learned the local language.

Case Study 4:
Role Reversal – Amanda and Simon

Overview

When Amanda has an amazing career opportunity that involves a move to Australia, decisions have to be made as Simon's career will always be in England. Simon wants to support Amanda as she is advancing quickly up the career ladder, but becoming a househusband has never been on his radar. However, he successfully overcomes social prejudices and remains fulfilled as he raises twins and pursues new and exciting activities.

Their Dual Career Journey

The setting: Amanda, who is British, joins a two-year graduate scheme with a private sector utilities company in the United Kingdom. She is posted to Indonesia for four months as part of the graduate training scheme. Here she gets a taste for working internationally. She meets Simon, who is also British, at a beach party while on holiday in India. The romance flourishes, and two years later they marry. By then Simon is in the police force and based in the Midlands region of the UK. It is difficult to move jobs in the police as each force is a separate entity. Amanda makes the first and only move for his career; she resigns and moves to the Midlands.

Moved for Simon's career.

The early years: Amanda finds a job with a multinational confectionary company in the Midlands. At this point she realizes that she is driven and ambitious and can get things done; the company recognizes this and she is put on the leadership track. As a result, she is offered opportunities to go overseas, but turns them down because they are undergoing IVF treatment and have to remain close to the hospital. In 2007, after five years of treatment, they have twins. During her maternity leave, the company

restructures and they have to move 'down south' to be just outside of London. By this time Simon has been promoted, becoming an inner-city detective dealing with serious crime, rape and murder. However, with Amanda's move, Simon finds a new job with a different police force. They sell their dream house and, with twins in tow, move close to London.

Moved for Amanda's career.

The big decision: Amanda returns to work after a year's maternity leave. They don't forget their common love for exploring and traveling, and one night over drinks discuss when they can start traveling again. They decide that it will not be for a few years as the twins are still young. However, not long after this conversation, Amanda is offered the opportunity to move to Australia as the company's HR Director for Australia and New Zealand. She quickly texts Simon with the news, saying, "Remember that conversation we had over drinks a few weeks ago? Do you fancy a move to Australia?" He texts back with, "Ya, OK." Of course, more conversations follow, and details need to be worked out, but the decision to go is agreed in minutes.

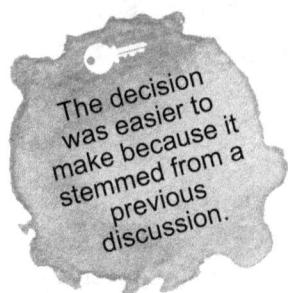

Discussed the future and agreed on what they wanted.

The decision was easier to make because it stemmed from a previous discussion.

By now, Simon is ready for a career break as working shift work and weekends leaves him with very little family time. They want to travel and it makes financial sense. Jobs within the police force are not transferable but generous with leave options and he isn't 100% happy in his job anyway. Simon applies for up to five years' parental leave and within three to four months of that fateful text

Simon considered his career options and chose the one that suited them best.

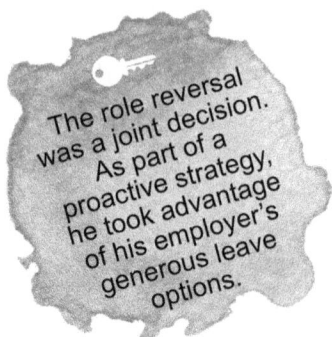

they are off to Australia with their 17-month-old twins.

The big shift: This role reversal marks a big shift for both of them. However, it is very much a joint decision, as Simon wants time with the children. He finds this new life has its own challenges. "To begin with, being at home every day with the kids wasn't easy," he says. The learning curve is steep as he learns to cook, clean the house, look after the kids and establish a new social network. It is hard, but living by the beach makes up for it. After a year of experimenting with role reversal, Simon tells Amanda, "I need a role if I am going to stay at home. I want you to focus on being a mum and leave the running of the household to me. Obviously you can help, but don't try to be a Super Mum, otherwise I have no role. When you are home, I want you to focus on being Mum, a wife and part of a family and not being distracted by doing the shopping and so on."

> The role reversal was a joint decision. As part of a proactive strategy, he took advantage of his employer's generous leave options.

> Simon communicated his feelings to Amanda and set about defining a role for himself.

"I am incredibly lucky and very grateful as he is still doing these things 10 years on," says Amanda. Not that Simon does not feel frustrated and down at times, but they have regular conversations about careers as well as about the challenges of being a stay-at-home dad. Simon finds it difficult to establish a social network. The other mums are friendly, but they never invite him to their homes for coffee. Curiously, the men who work are patronizing toward him because he does not have a job. They often make comments about how they wish they could spend time with their children. It takes Simon a while

> They had regular Dual Career Conversations.

to settle down to this new way of life, but once he finds his network of stay-at-home dads, they become good friends and he really starts to enjoy life in Australia.

The next hurdle: Simon enjoys playing golf, they have a good circle of friends and they have settled down in their respective roles as a family. At this point, Amanda's company is taken over by a manufacturing and processing conglomerate and Amanda is offered jobs in either Singapore or India. "We always make job decisions together; we didn't want to go to Singapore," recalls Amanda. "In fact, we would have liked to go to India, but we would have had to live in a compound with Simon as the only male and only non-Indian Accompanying Partner. We decided not to go."

> Simon recognized the social challenges and explored opportunities to overcome them.

> They made a shared decision not to accept Singapore or India.

By this time, Simon is an avid golfer and loves living in Australia. After much discussion, they agree that Amanda should leave the company and join a local retail company. This seems to work for about six months until Amanda's boss leaves. She then becomes very unhappy in her job. After a year she decides to leave the company. Now they are at a crossroads; do they return to the UK or do they look for another job abroad?

> Another shared decision.

The turning point: Within a week of Amanda leaving her job, they decide to get a jeep to explore Australia's Northern Territory with their four-year-old twins. As Amanda recalls, "Initially we were both devastated at the thought of having to leave Australia but decided to take the opportunity of my not

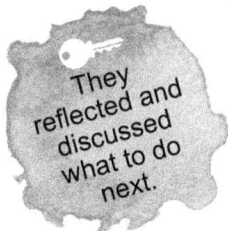

> They reflected and discussed what to do next.

working to explore and travel. We used the time driving round Australia to think, reflect and discuss what life we wanted as a family; did we want to continue to live in Australia or move on?" This trip marks the turning point for the couple.

Initially, the options are to either return to the UK or look for another job elsewhere. After lots of talking and driving, they agree that they like the lifestyle of living abroad, and financially it makes no sense to return to the UK. They don't know what the future holds for them except that they will move on elsewhere. Here in the Australian desert, they realize that blame would destroy their relationship. Under the stars, they agree on what Amanda calls "this bizarre thing we do once we have made a decision; we literally shake hands and say 'no blame, no regrets.'"

They made a decision and resolved not to blame each other should it go wrong.

Amanda explored opportunities. While they are on the road, Amanda is in contact with executive headhunters and is interviewed for jobs. After three months, it is Christmas. Switzerland is a possibility, and she flies to Zurich for the final interview, following which she agrees to start work at Easter.

On her return from Switzerland, they resume their road trip for another month, knowing that they will not be returning anytime soon.

Switzerland: They arrive in Switzerland and Amanda is now the regional head of organizational development for a multinational brewing and beverage company. The five years' parental leave for Simon is up and after discussion with Amanda, he makes the decision to leave the police force and continue their global lifestyle as a family. Simon really loves Switzerland, becoming a champion cyclist and an integral part of the Swiss cycling community. But

Amanda is not enjoying her role. She travels a lot, and the position proves to be very political and far removed from the actual business. Ultimately, she admits she hates her job. Much as Simon loves Switzerland, he is supportive and wants Amanda to be happy. Amanda tells me that Simon always says, "Three strikes and we leave. I want you to be happy in your job." Fortunately, there is a job for Amanda with the same company but based in Prague. This is the second time Simon leaves a country he has fallen in love with.

They made a shared decision regarding Simon's career.

Simon was supportive when Amanda did not like her job. Her job contentment was his top priority.

Prague: "Prague was not on his wish list of countries," says Amanda. However, both Amanda and Simon believe that comparing countries never helps, and it is more helpful to think *wherever you go is different, not better*. Prague is a very beautiful city, but the language is not easy and the variety of food is limited. Soon they discover that Prague offers them a great outdoor life of exploration and easy driving access to Germany, Croatia, Romania and Austria. The twins are now 13, so Amanda and Simon have more 'me time.' Amanda starts horse riding again and Simon starts to participate in triathlons; he is also cycling long distance to Kraków, Vienna and Berlin. "He is a fit machine. Everyone is in awe of him," says Amanda proudly. Likewise, he is equally proud of her and tells her how he is amazed at all she does and how articulate she is. "I love that he is so proud of me," Amanda continues. "We don't compete with each

They focused on the positive aspects of the location.

Mutual support and recognition of achievements.

other, and he is completely supportive of my career as I was of his in the past."

Their closeness as a couple is reflected even in their approach to their finances. "From the day we married, we had a joint account. If you can't share money, I don't understand the basis of marriage," says Amanda.

They followed the 'our' approach in more than just their careers.

This is their sixth year in Prague, where Amanda is a regional human resources director. The critical factor in any decision they make going forward will be their children's education.

What can we learn from Amanda and Simon's story?

> **GOLDEN RULE #2: MAKE SHARED DECISIONS**
>
> 1. They discuss every move. Although Simon no longer works, it is still a joint decision.
> 2. They agree jointly on which posting is good for Amanda's career and for them as a couple/family. For example, they do not accept a posting in India because it would be hard for Simon to live on a compound and be the only non-Indian male Accompanying Partner.

GOLDEN RULE #3: SET YOUR 'NO-GO' AREAS EARLY ON

1. Simon recognizes that Amanda needs to be happy in her job. "Three strikes and we leave."
2. Simon needs a role as a stay-at-home dad, and Amanda needs to allow him to be in charge of the house.
3. They determine not to blame each other for decisions they make, should they prove to be wrong, as this could destroy them. "No blame, no regrets," they said, shaking hands.
4. They are never competitive toward each other.

GOLDEN RULE #5: MAKE DUAL CAREER CONVERSATIONS A HABIT

1. They have career discussions regularly, especially each time there is a career change or a need to move to another country. But much depends on what is happening in their lives at the time.

Keys to Success

1. Making joint decisions about where to go next. Most of the time, the key factor was Amanda's job but not always. For example, they refused to go to India because they felt that a compound-living situation in a culture that was not used to stay-at-home dads would not work for them as a family. Now that the children are older, education considerations are the top priority in every move.

2. The roles and responsibilities within the marriage are clear. Although the role of Simon as a stay-at-home dad was initially challenging, they kept to it as he worked through the challenges. Simon also set about defining his role outside the home and chose cycling and triathlons.

3. They live by their mantra of 'shake hands, no regrets and no blame.' They both believe strongly that blaming each other would destroy their relationship. When a decision needs to be made, they make the best decision at a given moment and don't look back.

4. They share a love of exploration and travel from the earliest days of their relationship.

5. They are mutually supportive and appreciative of how each other contributes to making their lifestyle possible. They are proud and appreciative of each other's achievements – her career success and his cycling and triathlon achievements.

6. They intentionally look for what is fun and unique about living in a particular location. For example, the Czech language is not easy, but the countryside is beautiful and there is access to Europe by car, giving them much to explore.

7. Do not compare countries – "Wherever you go is different, not better."

8. A win for one must be experienced as a win for all. This becomes more important in the single career model as the non-working partner may feel that he/she is making all the sacrifices. They are living the life that they want.

9. They have an 'our' mindset toward career, lifestyle, finances (they have a joint bank account), exploration and travel, and their respective successes and achievements.

Case Study 5: Combination of Turn-Taking, Primary-Secondary and Role Reversal – Cielo and Charles

Overview

Cielo, from Barbados, and Charles, from Australia, meet in London in 2010. For Charles, an earlier experience of working in Cambodia has instilled in him a curiosity to live and work overseas. His next stop is London where he works in the field of communications for a human rights charity. Cielo studies accountancy in Edinburgh, and after graduation returns to Barbados to work for one of the Big Four professional services firms. Two years later, she moves to London with her company to gain more experience in the City. Interestingly, like Charles, a short volunteering stint – in her case with an NGO in Sierra Leone – leads her to a career pivot. Both agree that the support of the other enables them to explore different career options and take opportunities that they may otherwise have passed up.

Their Dual Career Journey

Their career journeys begin very differently. Charles arrives in London with high hopes that his experience in the Australian civil service, including his one-year stint in Cambodia, will stand him in good stead for a role in international development in London. With hindsight Charles admits, "I had overestimated my experience, which didn't translate well into the UK international development job market." This causes him to take on a variety of temporary roles. Through 'learning by doing,' he discovers new opportunities as a writer for an international development think tank.

Cielo's career, on the other hand, goes from strength to strength. She moves out from external audit to internal audit and risk management and also gains work experience with public listed companies. "I was succeeding on a path that I really didn't want, and I was always looking for ways to transition to development." In 2013, Cielo volunteers at a woman-led NGO in Sierra Leone. This further increases her interest in development and a desire to do more meaningful work.

Cielo explored opportunities for a change of career.

The perfect storm: During this period, Charles is thinking of applying for a job in Washington DC. By this time, they have been together for two and a half years. It is time for serious conversations that cover more than careers! Does Cielo want to accompany Charles to DC? "Obviously, we talked about what would happen if he got the job," she recalls. "We decided to take a leap of faith and move up a gear in our relationship," adds Charles. Cielo has some savings and sees this move to DC as a couple as an opportunity for a career reset or to segue into international development. In the spring of 2014, Charles moves to Washington DC to work for an international NGO as a writer/editor. Cielo joins him a few months later.

They had serious conversations about more than just their careers.

Life in DC: Life in the USA begins with a candid conversation between Cielo and the immigration officer at Dulles Airport about what brings her to the USA and what happens if the relationship doesn't work out! They are very much a couple but not married, which brings bureaucratic complications related to the work visa, healthcare and other administrative issues. This hastens their decision to marry.

Career pivot: Her volunteer experience in Sierra Leone has left a lasting impression on Cielo and a determination to use her skills in banking and finance in the development sector. The move to

DC offers Cielo the opportunity to explore how and where she could pivot. Although she does fleetingly toy with the idea of working for a previous employer in DC, she decides to focus on doing something different. Fortuitously, a former classmate offers Cielo a job opportunity in her economic consultancy practice. She seizes this as a chance to use her analytical skills in the areas of research, policy and governance work. In 2015, just after they book a date for the wedding, Cielo lands a short-term consultancy with an international organization.

Cielo sought job opportunities...

... and continued looking for something that suited her even better.

Plans changed by circumstances: By 2017, Charles is not happy in his job and so after some discussion they decide to move back to Australia. They buy their tickets and arrange to have their household goods packed and loaded for shipment. Just as they are winding down their lives in DC, Cielo gets an offer of a staff position with an international organization in the USA. In fact, she receives not one but two offers from the many applications they made when faced with the prospect of returning to Australia.

Discussed another big decision.

The job offer presents an opportunity for Cielo. Do they do a U-turn? Charles describes their decision to accept and return to the USA as "a no brainer; a staff position at an international organization fulfills one of her career aspirations to work in development and I was very proud of her." They proceed with their plans and go to Australia for six months before returning to the USA.

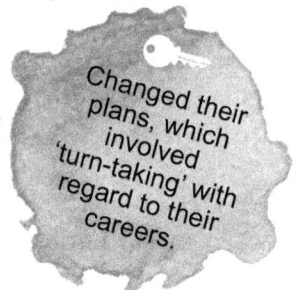

Changed their plans, which involved 'turn-taking' with regard to their careers.

By this time, Charles has quit his job, as planned; he decides to establish himself as a freelance writer and editor on his return to the USA. This shift into establishing himself as a freelance writer/editor provides them with more flexibility to work and live anywhere in the future.

Recognized the long-term benefits of flexibility.

On the move again: In 2019 it is time to move again, this time to Paris where Cielo works for an intergovernmental organization doing research and policy. Charles continues as a freelance writer. Although they have only been there for a year, they spend a lot of time reflecting on and discussing what kind of life they want. Increasingly, as mid-career transition approaches, they are thinking more about the kind of life they want in the future. Up to now, the main driver in their decision-making has been their respective careers; now their focus is changing to life itself.

Ongoing career discussions.

Discussed life choices as well as careers.

The future: "I have been more itinerant than I want to be, so setting up a home base is becoming more urgent now," says Cielo. Charles describes it as "having to be more grown up, putting roots down somewhere and owning our first home." It will most likely be Australia. They are emphatic they will not remain 'at home' forever; they will move again. However, more immediately, they feel the need to have a home base to move out from in the future.

Reflecting on their decisions: What struck Cielo when they first met in London was how excited Charles was about his job, and it was eye opening for her to see the different ways that one could work. "My only exposure was in the financial services sector when we became a couple. Charles gave me the extra push to make the leap and take a placement in Sierra Leone."

Cielo continues. "Our approach to career is not just about money. It is mainly about 'what does this opportunity mean for me or Charles?' We were already on our way to Australia; I received the job offer as our shipment was being packed.

Give and take.

But it was an opportunity for me, so we made that U-turn. We initially moved to DC for Charles, and I came without a job and a visa; that was an opportunity for him." There is give and take for the greater good.

Charles is very clear that, from the beginning, Cielo is the higher-income earner and will be for the foreseeable future. "Certain professions just pay better. I want to do more writing but that is not going to be earning us a whole bunch," he says pragmatically.

Open discussions, with no ego.

He continues, "When we met, Cielo was a high-income earner but respectful of my career. If we had had ego clashes, we would have failed quite early on in our relationship. We have always talked with openness and lack of ego from the start."

Given their constant reflection and discussion about what they want out of life, coupled with the ability to balance vision and opportunity, they are confident that things will fall into place. "He is the champion of my career," adds Cielo as we conclude the interview.

What can we learn from Cielo and Charles's story?

◎ **GOLDEN RULE #5: MAKE DUAL CAREER CONVERSATIONS A HABIT**

1. This was part and parcel of their relationship right from when they first met. Cielo was struck by how excited Charles was about his work.

◎ **GOLDEN RULE #2: MAKE SHARED DECISIONS**

1. They discuss every move together.
2. They have a common long-term goal of setting up a home base as a couple.
3. They make career decisions based on 'the opportunity that the role offers her/him.'

Keys to Success

1. Seizing career opportunities to increase career flexibility and not be pigeon-holed. This included returning to Washington DC even after their household goods were being packed for Australia when Cielo got the job at an international organization; and Cielo leaving London without a job and visa to join Charles in Washington.

2. Cielo and Charles are mutually supportive of each other, acting as anchor and push.

3. Charles's decision to become a freelance writer/editor has provided them with much more flexibility to go wherever the opportunities are for Cielo in the future. They are evolving into a primary-secondary career model.

4. Identifying their long-term shared goal, which for Cielo and Charles is setting up a home base somewhere.

Case Study 6: Non-Traditional, Same-Sex Couple – Chuck and Chen

Overview

Chuck and Chen would consider themselves as following a double primary model. When they met, both were pursuing thriving careers. However, in reality, the combination of their being a same-sex couple and internationally mobile has resulted till now in a primary-secondary model.

Their Dual Career Journey

Chuck, an American, describes himself as a global gypsy; this means going where the 'cool gig' is. He made up his mind, age 16, that this is what he would be when he grew up. Twenty-seven years and nine countries later, he is still aiming for the next 'cool gig' that will enrich him personally and professionally. This has resulted in a rich suite of career experience and expertise in mergers and acquisitions, compensation and total rewards, organizational development, and scaling start-ups to become mature businesses. As Reid Hoffman says in *The Start-Up of You*, "For many people '20 years of experience' is really one year of experience repeated 20 times." In Chuck's case, it has been more than 20 years of different career experiences. The last 13 years of the journey have been with his partner, Chen, a fashion stylist, who is 16 years younger. The journey has been challenging at times – for one, or both of them – because of immigration limitations due to non-acceptance of LGBTQIA+ couples, and this has been compounded by passport restrictions due to nationality (Chen is from China). Much of the journey has been a quest for a place

Chuck was flexible, being willing to go wherever the 'cool gig' was. Created career assets.

where they can blossom and where both can be employed. This has not been easy.

Finding love in Shanghai: Chuck meets Chen while working in Shanghai with a major consulting company and Chen is working as a fashion stylist for companies like Vogue. In 2013, Chuck changes jobs to work with a major local business. "It wasn't that great for me working at this Chinese

> Chuck made the initial sacrifice to enable Chen's career to flourish.

technology company, but as Chen's career was flourishing, I knew I could make it work for us," says Chuck. By doing so, they are able to accommodate two careers (the *double primary* model). However, by 2015, it is time for another career move, as another cool gig is calling. This time they are off to Amsterdam.

Amsterdam, the best city in the world… but: "Amsterdam is one of the best cities in the world for same-sex couples," says Chuck. "The Dutch are very tolerant, the lifestyle is great and gays are welcome." But there is one huge drawback: Chen cannot work here because of work permit restrictions. All their decision-making

> They established a 'personal GPS' to guide their decision-making.

is guided by what Chuck refers to as their 'GPS.' Their GPS, he explains, is, "a) what will make us mutually advance – there must be co-equal benefit; b) the decision must put us in a better space than before, and c) we must learn and be enriched by this experience."

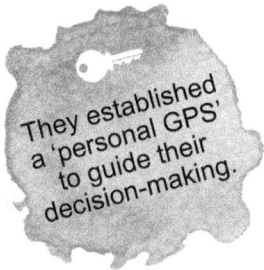

New York City and marriage: In 2016, they mutually agree to move to New York City, where they are married. Chen then enrolls at the Fashion Institute of Technology and the Parsons School of Design. He loves living in one of the fashion capitals of the world and having access to some of the

> They made a shared decision on how to combine Chuck's career with further opportunities for Chen.

best creative minds. Chuck works for a multinational consumer internet company.

Next Stop, Lausanne: But all too soon it is time for another move as in 2018 Chuck is offered a position as Vice President of Total Rewards for a global organization. This opportunity, which is too good to refuse, takes them to Lausanne, Switzerland. However, Lausanne proves to be challenging because of its lack of acceptance of LGBTQIA+ couples. Chen feels very uncomfortable and is happy just to stay home, which puts a strain on the relationship. Although Chuck feels guilty that Chen is making such a career sacrifice, he finds it difficult to understand why Chen isn't considering a career pivot. A compromise needs to be struck, but it is not easy to find a location that meets all three criteria of their GPS. After much

> Lausanne proved to be tougher than expected for both of them, requiring another shared decision to move on.

discussion, combined with Chuck's increasing ethical unease with the tobacco industry (since he is working for a tobacco company) and the onset of Covid-19, they decide jointly that it is time to move on.

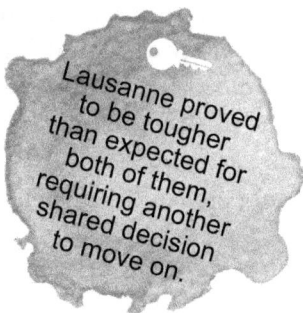

> They had to recalibrate and reflect on the best way to address their career challenges.

Back to Amsterdam and recalibration: They are now back in Amsterdam where they feel accepted as part of the community and are taking the time to think, reflect and discuss their next steps. Having made their relationship the priority, Chuck is looking for a new job while Chen considers how he can resume his career in fashion. Chuck is thinking that it may mean going back to Shanghai where Chen is a citizen and faces no restrictions, so that he can resume his career, which has been on hold, except for

> Open to changing career models.

some remote work, since they left New York. Moreover, there is a 16-year age gap between them. This puts them at very different points in their career journeys. Hence, they have had to search for a country that will allow them to grow professionally, is tolerant of their sexual orientation and can provide equal benefit to each of them.

What can we learn from Chuck and Chen's story?

◎ **GOLDEN RULE #2: MAKE SHARED DECISIONS**

1. During the interview, Chuck used the word 'mutual' many times – mutually beneficial, mutually decided.
2. They established a mutually agreed GPS, which guides their decision-making.

◎ **GOLDEN RULE #5: MAKE DUAL CAREER CONVERSATIONS A HABIT**

Chuck and Chen have three types of Dual Career Conversations:

1. The episodic check-in conversations when nothing in particular is happening.
2. Rebuttal conversations when there are career tensions between them.
3. Constant conversations when facing important strategic decisions about next steps and/or the future.

Keys to Success

This Case Study demonstrates the use of three career models to navigate career continuation and coordination.

1. They were a *double primary Dual Career Couple* when they met in Shanghai, each pursuing their own career trajectory. When they became a couple, Chuck took up a job with a large Chinese technology company in order to continue the double primary model.
2. When they moved to Amsterdam, their model switched to the *primary-secondary model* because of work permit restrictions.
3. Should they decide to move back to Shanghai in the near future, they would be following *the turn-taking model.*

The changes reflect the fact that different stages of the life and career cycle of couples cause them to choose different models.

LGBTQIA+ couples who are internationally mobile, like Chuck and Chen, face the additional challenge of finding national cultures that are accepting of their sexual orientation, and where immigration rules allow both partners to work. For example, it is easier for a couple who are both EU citizens to work in Europe. Hence, the degree of challenge varies for each couple depending on personal history.

What Can We Learn about Successful Dual Careers from These Case Studies?

The stories of these couples were selected because they have all relocated between three and six times as a couple. Certain commonalities and Keys to Success emerge, although each couple has chosen a different career model. None of the couples would say that it all worked perfectly. With hindsight, they may have made some different decisions, but what they have in common is that they all intuitively adhered to the same three Golden Rules (out of the eight listed in *Chapters 1* to *3*). It is evident that these three Golden Rules are clearly crucial to the successful management of their Dual Careers.

The Three Key Golden Rules

1. Have regular Dual Career Conversations.

2. Respect each Other's no-go zones.

3. Make shared decisions.

In addition to the Three Key Golden Rules, these six Case Studies clearly demonstrate the importance of the following:

- **Career prioritization**: If a couple at the outset of their relationship have an equal commitment to their career and their relationship, then career prioritization must be discussed, especially if international mobility is part of their career trajectory and/or plan for one or both of them. Career prioritization has to be discussed very early in the relationship. Robert and Rosemary learned from their first experience in the US that careers have to be managed, otherwise one partner will bear the brunt of it. In their case, Robert felt acutely underemployed. You will recall that in each of the Case Studies, the couples chose different career models and that the career models changed depending on their life stage, career opportunities and skill set.

- **A win for all**: For Dual Career Couples to be successful, decisions have to be shared and the experience of relocation from one country to another has to be experienced as a win for all. Amanda from Case Study 4 is the sole breadwinner, but Simon has carved out a role for himself as a champion athlete and stay-at-home dad. Recalibration is needed when the experience is not a win for all, as shown in the Case Study of Chuck and Chen.

- **Career management**: The careers of both partners have to be managed in light of the agreements you have reached as a couple. For example, Maja knew right at the start of their relationship that Henrik working for the Swedish Ministry for Foreign Affairs meant a peripatetic way of life for them. Hence, they agree that he would only accept postings where she could work, and they would alternate between an overseas and home posting so that Maja would be able to work. After their first posting in Japan, she realized that moving to the public sector would be better for her career because of the generous leave of absence policies. This meant that her position would be held open for a fixed period of time, and on her return, she would be able to start work almost immediately, thus avoiding the 'stop-start syndrome' that many Accompanying Partners complain about. As their assignments are generally for three years, she deliberately chose to work on projects that were timebound or phased to maximize her employment prospects and minimize the impact on her employers.

  Keeping an eye out for opportunities that increase one's career flexibility is another important aspect of career management for the globally mobile professional.

Points for Reflection

Which strategies from the Case Studies can we, as a couple, apply to help us manage our careers better?

PART TWO

APPLYING THE CARE CODE TO ADDRESS THE DILEMMA

Chapter 5

Putting CARE into the Dual Career

In this chapter you will learn:

- How to have productive CARE conversations.
- How to use The CARE Code and exercises to help solve Dual Career dilemmas.

"Every choice that we make has its risks and its downsides. But these reflections may help you reshape your choices and lessen some of the most serious risks – regrets that come from acquiescing to one partner's decisions, or not making any decisions."
Jennifer Petriglieri

Why Have CARE Conversations?

Do you remember the stories of Anjana, Amelia and Camilla in the previous chapters? None of them had in-depth conversations with their partner, which resulted in short-term decisions that caused them angst. Life as a Dual Career Couple is complex. As the Case Studies so clearly demonstrate, there is no quick fix, magic formula or one-size-fits-all approach. However, the question remains. How do we attain the careers and life we aspire to?

Sometimes, a career choice may involve a life-changing move for your partner, you and/or your family. It warrants more than a quick yes or no from one's partner. How can you decide to make a career move without ever considering how this piece will fit into the jigsaw of life? All too often, we accept the career opportunity that is presented to us as the golden key that will unlock the treasure trove, except that it proves to be Pandora's box. In other words, we react without a full understanding of the consequences because we have not established a habit of having regular Dual Career Conversations with our partner.

Many couples only discuss their career plans when a challenge arises or when there is an impending move; for example, when one partner is approached by the company to relocate to another geographic location. But how common is it that a couple make it a habit to have a thoughtful, reflective conversation about how *our* careers fit into the mosaic of the life that *we* want and dream of? For most of us, we suppose that somehow the disparate parts will fall into place and a beautiful life will magically come into focus quite by chance or good fortune. This is where having regular CARE conversations becomes essential. Learning to build this habit of regular conversations will help you develop an 'our' mindset. It may just be the magic you need for a 'happily ever after' life!

What Is a CARE Conversation?

CARE Conversations are important and necessary. They are an invitation to co-create a combined existence, a partnership of mutual support. It is challenging to combine two distinct career paths, so when push comes to shove it becomes a choice between *yours* or *mine*. Often, as we have seen in previous chapters, it results in an imbalance, where one partner takes most of the risks and downsides. CARE Conversations provide the opportunity to reframe the dilemma from mine or yours to *ours*. Our own story and the Case Studies show that there are different ways to combine life and careers on the move. Otherwise, Camilla's story is a familiar refrain.

Simply put, CARE Conversations are discussions couples have about their careers, their long-term plans and the kind of life they desire as a family unit, using The CARE Code to help guide their discussions. These types of conversations can be uncomfortable for some couples and lead to conflict, especially when there are competing priorities. The CARE Code helps you to prioritize and organize your thinking first as *individuals* and then as a *couple,* as you think about how *my* career becomes *our* careers. Both partners must CARE to make it work.

After all, any career move that entails moving to a new location will impact the whole family. Furthermore, such conversations have to become a habit, just as career conversations are a regular feature of corporate life. In the Case Studies you followed in the previous chapter, we saw that one of the Keys to Success for all the couples was making this kind of CARE Conversation a habit.

The Seeds of The CARE Code

The CARE Code started as our intuitive approach to wrestling with the dilemmas we had as a bi-racial Dual Career Couple at the outset of our marriage. Where to make our lives – my country or his? How would we accommodate our careers and live the lives to which we aspired? Through our sometimes-heated discussions, our reflective and yet animated conversations helped us to work through many dilemmas, as a result of which the seeds of what is now The CARE Code were unwittingly sown. Together, we stepped out as a partnership into a future that was largely unknown. All we knew was that we wanted to forge into the unknown together.

First and foremost, we had to decide where we would live our lives as a married couple as I am Singaporean and Graham is British. Since Graham was already working when I graduated, we decided to start off in England for the time being. We agreed that we would only move to Singapore if our careers took us there as Graham did not want to spend the rest of his life in Asia.

Our no-go zones and non-negotiables

I spent the first five years of our marriage working out what I wanted to do, wondering where I would find satisfaction and be paid what I was worth. Although I was always 'in employment' I searched for 'something more.' When I finally decided on journalism, I was faced with a dilemma: our life goal of using our vacation time for traveling clashed with the 14-day vacation policy. At the time, Graham was an academic and had six weeks of vacation a year. This forced us to think very hard about our no-go zones, my non-negotiables and Graham's. It seemed I had a choice; I could either pursue my career goals or fulfill our dreams of travel while we had the opportunity. After much discussion, soul searching and angst on my part, we chose travel. I forfeited my writing dream. Our no-go zones were fairly easy to agree on as our orientation to life was similar:

- Family first (initially as a couple and then as a family when the children arrived).

- No long-distance relationship.

Our next Dual Career dilemma crept up on us toward the end of Graham's contract in Singapore with the publication of my book *We Remember: Cameos of Pioneer Life*. It was an attempt to capture the colonial era from an Asian perspective, and, with its publication came offers to write other books and the need to be based in Singapore. By then we also had a three-month-old daughter, Antonia. Now we were faced with the dilemma of career prioritization – his or mine? Was it my turn at last? Graham was totally supportive. However, I did not want our children to be raised by a nanny. We wanted one of us to be at home during their early years. Family would come first. Again, after much discussion, I reluctantly agreed that for now, while our daughter was still a baby, Graham's career would have priority. This meant that we would go wherever the opportunity took us. It was a shared decision. Although I was sometimes irked by what could have been, there was really very little comeback for me because Graham had been happy for my career to take priority. I knew that if I were the breadwinner, I would have huge responsibility. In the end I chose freedom. Freedom to carve my own niche.

This choice took us to Manila, the Philippines, where Graham joined the Asian Development Bank as the English language consultant. Here we decided that, since I was already on a career break, we should have our second child. The date for my return to work was set the day I decided I would be a stay-at-home mum until Alastair started pre-school. All told, I took nearly four years off. The day he started pre-school, I returned to work.

Because of the value we placed on putting our family first and not being separated as a family, mine was the secondary career for many years. In fact, when Graham was offered a position at the International Monetary Fund in Washington DC, we nearly turned it down because our son was entering sixth form in the UK and, initially, he could not get a place at Washington International School as it was full.

What worked for us also works for other Dual Career Couples

Looking back on our lives I realized we did three things consistently:

1. We had regular Dual Career Conversations, which covered our thoughts, fears and aspirations.
2. Our two no-go zones guided all our decision-making.
3. We made shared decisions.

When I was conducting the interviews for the Case Studies (see *Chapter 4, A Win for All*), a clear pattern emerged.

- Establishing a modus operandi was essential to each couple's ability to navigate Dual Careers and international mobility. Crucially, these couples addressed career prioritization. Now they had guidance as to which opportunities to pursue and which ones not to.

- All the couples had regular Dual Career Conversations, respected each other's no-go zones and made shared decisions. It was clear that these were habits they practiced regularly, and intensely when career and/or life related matters needed urgent discussion. Your needs and circumstances may change over time but if you have Dual Career Conversations regularly you will be able to anticipate the challenges and proactively partner to take action.

- The power of shared decisions is imperative for creating a win for all. According to leading theorist and clinical psychologist Richard Ryan, autonomy is one of the three basic psychological needs of human beings. It provides an individual with a sense of control and agency of their circumstances. A lack of autonomy felt by the Accompanying Partner can lead to feelings of frustration and anger, as well as unfairness that the career privilege rests repeatedly with one partner.

The combination of high-impact mobility and Dual Careers makes for a roller-coaster ride for couples who are committed to both their careers and each other and their families. Therefore, you have to care enough to make it work.

The CARE Code

How does The CARE Code help?

The CARE Code provides a framework that will help you to:

- Clarify your own career goals and aspirations.
- Have productive Dual Career Conversations with your partner.
- Discuss and agree as a couple on your no-go zones and determine your career prioritization.
- Plan your career paths together, while considering other factors such as family.
- Explore opportunities.
- Make shared decisions.

In many ways, The CARE Code is the fruit of several decades of working with internationally mobile Dual Career Couples. It is based on a thousand conversations and countless observations along the way. It is also the result of many years of research, study and practical application. But it was finally birthed when I saw the connection between our intuitive approach and the Keys to Success in the Case Studies you saw in *Chapter 4, A Win for All.*

The CARE Code is a simple tool designed to help Dual Career Couples have a systematic, constructive conversation about what matters to them beyond the purely pragmatic issues of financial rewards, summer camps, travel schedules and time with family. It will show you how to proactively partner as you navigate life and careers.

CARE is the mnemonic for **Clarify**, **Assess**, **Refocus** and **Explore**. Use The CARE Code to mitigate any blind spots you may have and to expand your focus beyond the practicalities to what will allow you both to thrive in your professional and personal lives.

The CARE Code

**Use The CARE Code
To Solve Dual Career Dilemmas**

C	A	R	E
Step One:	Step Two:	Step Three:	Step Four:
Clarify	**A**ssess	**R**efocus	**E**xplore

- Decide on what matters to you individually and as a couple.
- Agree on the priorities for your careers and life together.
- Communicate regularly.

- Agree on no-go zones.
- Anticipate challenges that may arise.
- Make shared decisions.

- Listen attentively to each other.
- Respect no-go zones.
- Repair as needed.

- Research thoroughly your options and check assumptions.
- Proactively partner with each other, your organization and other significant stakeholders.
- Take action.

The couples in the Case Studies had largely followed the framework presented in The CARE Code. This had enabled them to reach agreement on the key principles and priorities for their careers and relationship. In other words, they had used The CARE Code to establish what really mattered to them and their modus operandi.

Case Study 1: Turn-Taking – Robert and Rosemary

1. No long-distance relationship.
2. Never make decisions that would hurt the other's career.
3. Manage your respective careers.
4. Plan ahead where possible.

Case Study 2: Double Primary – Melissa and Christian

1. Clarity about priorities – made the decision early on in the relationship that career was a priority for both of them, even if this meant having a long-distance relationship for a time.
2. Willing to have a long-distance relationship if necessary. But look for opportunities to move closer geographically.
3. After starting a family, they would only move to locations where both of them could work.

Case Study 3: Primary-Secondary – Maja and Henrik

1. Avoid a long-distance relationship.
2. Only apply to postings where Maja could work.
3. Alternate overseas and home postings so Maja could resume her career more easily.

Case Study 4: Role Reversal – Amanda and Simon

1. No blame, no regrets once a shared decision is made.
2. Three strikes and we leave if unhappy with the job situation.
3. They agreed Simon would have a clearly defined role, especially as he does not work.

Case Study 5: Combination of Turn-Taking, Primary-Secondary and Role Reversal – Cielo and Charles

1. Make career decisions based on the opportunity that the role offers her/him.
2. Plan toward establishing a home base in the next few years.

Case Study 6: Non-Traditional, Same-Sex Couple – Chuck and Chen

1. Their decision-making is guided by their personal GPS:
   a. There must be co-equal benefit in each move.
   b. The decision to move must put them in a better space than before.
   c. They must learn and be enriched by the particular experience.

These couples designed a personal compass to help them navigate the map of life together. Most importantly and crucially they discussed how career prioritization would work for them. Now they had their GPS and roadmap.

How to Have a CARE Conversation

In contrast to the Case Study couples, many couples have hardly left the starting line when it comes to discussing what matters. Yet they seem surprised by the impact of their decision to accompany their partner or have become tired of the 'stop-start' syndrome that many an Accompanying Partner faces as he/she moves from location to location. And some are angry and frustrated at having become a 'professional follower' without discussing their own career ambitions with their partner.

CARE Conversations can often be uncomfortable and bring out strong emotions between the couple. As a result, it becomes all too easy to focus on the practicalities. But for effective CARE Conversations, refrain from discussing the carpool, work travel schedules and so on for a few minutes. Instead, focus on understanding each other's feelings, fears, anxieties, expectations. The practicalities of life can be onerous, but with careful planning, juggling and outsourcing, most of the crinkles can be ironed out. In contrast, without open discussions, feelings of resentment, unmet expectations and fears can derail the best of relationships. Often, it is our emotions that drive our thinking. Jennifer Petriglieri, in her book *Couples That Work*, suggests that discussing your fears as a couple can serve as both an early warning signal that your relationship is entering dangerous waters as well as enabling pre-emptive action before you hit the rocks. Forewarned is forearmed.

CARE Conversations are also a great opportunity to 'repair' and refocus. *Repair* is a concept defined by John Gottman, world renowned relationship therapist, researcher and founder of The Love Lab, as "any statement or action – silly or otherwise – that prevents negativity from escalating out of control." Repair in this context is about getting back on track. Gottman purposely uses the word 'any' to allow you to create or discover repair strategies unique to you as a couple.

If you have never done this before as a couple, you will initially have to invest the time to discuss issues you have never talked about before or in a long time. CARE Conversations have to become part of your thinking and decision-making process. Once they have become a habit, this type of conversation needs to happen only two or three times a year. As in the Case Studies, you will recall that when there is an impending career decision or if one or both of you are encountering challenges at work, the conversations could be daily. Often life's triggers and checkpoints will serve as natural jump-off points to re-evaluate and recalibrate. For example, you may be offered a promotion that requires a relocation; your partner may think it is time for a job switch, be approached by a competitor or want to try out his/her entrepreneurial wings.

Essentials for CARE Conversations

1. Make each other feel safe.

2. Listen well. Did you know that research indicates that the average individual only listens for 17 seconds without interrupting? According to Nicky and Sila Lee, authors of *The Marriage Course*, there is no one more important to listen to than your partner, and the art of effective listening is a skill we can ALL learn, but it takes time and intention.

3. Work together to make it happen.

4. Commit to making time for deep and meaningful discussion.

5. Appreciate each other.

Avoid the Four Horsemen

The most satisfying conversations occur when both parties are willing to listen and to be honest and open. Unsurprisingly, with hindsight everything becomes clearer and on occasion may be filled with regret. For CARE Conversations to be productive, the Four Horsemen of the Apocalypse – Criticism, Contempt, Defensiveness and Stonewalling – have to be locked in the stables. This is the metaphor developed by John Gottman to describe communication styles that can be disruptive to relationships. At all costs, do not blame or be accusative or sarcastic. Here are the three Cs for designing a partnership that works:

1. Communication

2. Commitment

3. Collaboration

However, we are only human, so we make mistakes and say the wrong thing; sometimes we are selfish, and so conflict with our nearest and dearest is inevitable. If the CARE Conversation is not going well, you would be well advised to adopt one of the following approaches in order to manage the situation.

1. The Repair Remote Control

The Repair Remote Control, developed by John Gottman, will help to de-escalate conflict in your CARE conversations.

Imagine repair attempts as buttons on a TV remote control. If the conversation goes awry, you can press a metaphorical button, as follows:

Rewind (Sorry)
- "Can I try again?"
- "I messed up."
- "How can I make things better?"
- "I'm sorry."

Fast Forward (Get to Yes)
- "I agree with part of what you're saying."
- "Let's find a compromise."
- "What are your concerns?"

Pause (I Need to Calm Down)
- "Can we take a break from this conversation for now?"
- "Please be gentler with me."
- "I am starting to feel flooded."

Stop (Stop Action!)
- "Give me a moment."
- "Let's agree to disagree."
- "We are getting off track."

Record (I appreciate)
- "That is a good point."
- "I know this isn't your fault."
- "I love you."

Microphone/Voice Command (I feel)
- "That hurt my feelings."
- "I feel defensive. Can you rephrase that?"
- "I'm getting worried."

2. HALT

HALT the conversation if you have to. HALT is an acronym used by counselors when dealing with chemical dependency. It originates from the Alcoholics Anonymous publication, *Living Sober*. It's a useful reminder when it comes to CARE Conversations, especially the thorny ones or if you see one of the 'four horsemen' approaching.

- **H is for hunger**. Some people, and I am one of them, get incredibly cranky and distracted when they feel hungry.

- **A is for anger**. Stop to reflect on what is making you angry. Take time out to regulate your emotions before continuing the discussion.

- **L is for loneliness**. In this particular instance, it may translate into feeling alone within the partnership. For example, if up to now you have felt that you have been taking on the lion's share of parenting and your requests for a more balanced parental load have gone unheard, you may feel lonely in your partnership. Or if every international move to date has been because of his/her job and you have had to 'stop and start' again. Discuss this with your partner when you can do this without being angry.

- **T is for tiredness**. It is never a good idea to have important discussions that are cognitively and emotionally taxing when one or both of you are sleep deprived, stressed or exhausted.

Exercises to Kickstart Your CARE Conversations

CARE Conversations are not meant to be burdensome, accusative or interrogative. They are conversations between two people who love each other and co-create a life together. Some couples have this conversation on long walks in the countryside. Others choose their favorite dinner restaurant or Saturday mornings over coffee and croissants. This can be hard to do, especially if you have a young family, so time has to be intentionally carved out; otherwise, it will easily dissipate into the hurly-burly of daily life, laundry and the school run. Why not try something as simple as turning off your phone, snuggling on the sofa with a glass of wine or sitting on the terrace enjoying the starlit sky and simply talking to each other? Do what works for you as a couple but create a space for this intentional conversation.

Refer to your notes on the Points for Reflection at the end of each chapter in this book and begin your discussions. You could even read the stories from *Chapters 2* and *3* over dinner; this can often spark lively conversations. A good starting point would be a discussion on Common Pitfalls.

I have included exercises below that you can use in your CARE Conversations. Exercises 1 to 5 focus on integrating your careers and life as a couple/family on the move. Exercise 6 helps you prepare for a career conversation with HR or your manager. More exercises are available on my website www.yvonnequahe.com.

Exercise 1: Spot the Common Pitfalls

> *Aim: To provide greater clarity as to which Common Pitfalls apply to your situation and how to address them going forward.*

This exercise will help you understand which Common Pitfalls you have experienced or are experiencing. It will also offer you the opportunity to share your perspective and listen to your partner's. Refer to *Chapters 1* and *3* about the Common Pitfalls that arise.

1. Read each Common Pitfall aloud to your partner. See the *Quick Reference Guide.*

2. If the Common Pitfall applies, discuss it together, ask clarifying questions and practice active listening. See examples of clarifying questions below.

3. Pay attention to your feelings.

4. Make a note of your answers.

5. Once you have identified the relevant *Common Pitfalls*, make sure you discuss them together and decide where you need to refocus. What action steps will you both take?

Here are examples of clarifying questions you can ask each other for six of the Common Pitfalls:

Common Pitfalls	Clarifying Questions
You readily agree to follow because you are currently not vested in your own career.	Are you clear about your career goals? What are they?
You don't take sufficient time to think about the implications of the move for you.	Is an international assignment something either of you wants to pursue as a career goal? What are your no-go zones?
You don't discuss your career continuity and coordination, which leads to one partner having to 'stop and start' with each move.	If you are already on assignment, are you experiencing 'stop and start' fatigue? How will you manage career continuation and coordination going forward?
You underestimate the cost.	Have you assessed the emotional and career cost of your move? What are these costs? Don't forget to consider the emotional costs of the decision, especially for the Accompanying Partner.
You don't fully understand the unintended consequences of role reversal.	Are you emotionally equipped to handle the role reversal? What do you need to do differently?
You assume that your role is to follow and that your career is automatically the secondary one.	Are you feeling short changed? If so, how can you rectify this? (Strong emotions of resentment and anger may require professional help.)

Exercise 2: Learning from the Past to Inform the Future

> *Aim: To understand and learn from your experiences as you think about where to go next as a couple/family.*

Choose two locations you have been posted to in the past. One which you think went well and another where it was more challenging.

Identify what mindset you had, what actions you took and what made this assignment go so well. Do the same for the location that you found challenging.

Families who have used this exercise have found it useful. One parent said: "It gave me an inroad to including the children in these conversations. Behaviors have not been great this posting as we have all struggled to settle in. By enabling the children to say what went well, what they enjoyed about the posting, what they found hard, what we should try to do more of/less of, etc., they are offered a semi-structured opportunity to let it all out!"

Discuss what made the difference and what you can apply moving forward.

What went well	What did not go well
Country: (e.g. Kenya)	Country: (e.g. Austria)

Exercise 3: Through the Looking Glass

Aim: To help couples clarify and assess what matters to them and the kind of life they want together.

Here are some questions to help you reflect on the life and career that you want and hopefully avoid the typical *Common Pitfalls*. Following the questions, you will find a template where you can note down and categorize your thoughts. Ask your partner to do the same.

- What kind of career do I want? Think of your career trajectory.
- What is important to me?
- What is the life that I want?
- What are my concerns about the future?
- How have we prioritized each other's career?
- What career model would I like?
- What expectations do I have of my partner in relation to both our careers?
- How has my culture/upbringing affected how I think about career, family, roles and responsibilities?
- What are my no-go zones? (For example, are there countries that I don't want to live and work in? Do I want to be near – how near – my aging parents?)

Exercise 3: My Reflections

What are my core values?

What are my fears?

What are my no-go zones?

How does my culture affect the way I view my career?

What are my career and life expectations?

What roles are important to me in life? What would happen if these roles changed?

Discuss your answers using The CARE Code.

Exercise 4: Windows of Opportunity

> *Aim: To identify the locations that will be experienced as a win for both partners.*

If you are already working for an organization, you can explore opportunities that fit with your career design.

1. Download and print two copies of the list of office locations of your respective organizations. If you are a self-initiated expatriate, print out a map of the world.

2. Using a red, green and blue pen, go through the list of countries marking them as follows:

- **Red:** no-go countries – meaning I don't want to live and work there.

- **Green:** countries I would consider/like an assignment in.

- **Blue:** boundaries beyond which you are not willing to go, because of the need for proximity to home, adult children, family, aging parents, etc.

3. Your partner can do likewise for his/her organization. Once you have each completed the list, compare your countries and discuss your choices. This may take some time to complete as you may need to do some preliminary research – for example, into work permit regulations and local employment opportunities. Check assumptions you make about certain destinations too.

4. Then draw up a list of possible locations to consider based on the countries you have marked **green**.

You will then be able to use this list when considering or positioning yourself for future job opportunities, and/or when having a Dual Career Conversation with your boss. You could also use this list as a basis for research on what the work permit regulations are and what job opportunities there are for the Accompanying Partner.

Exercise 5: Choosing the Right Time

> *Aim: To discuss and explore together when would be the optimal time, given career/life cycles, to pursue an international assignment or to return to a home base.*

Use the exercise below if:

1. You are considering a move right now.

2. You are planning a move in the future and have a specific location(s) in mind.

Complete this table:

If we move now, what would complicate this move?	If we move now, what would facilitate this move?
For example: aging parents who need support.	The kids are still in elementary school

After you have completed this table, ask your partner to do so too and then discuss the results.

Exercise 6: Preparing for a Dual Career CARE Conversation with Your Manager

> *Aim: To prepare for constructive conversations with your employer to leverage opportunities in line with OUR goals/priorities.*

You can engage with your employer in various ways. One formal route will be via performance review conversations where growth and career development conversations take place. Use these as opportunities to align or refocus your career experiences. It is always a good idea to build a variety of career skills that can be used in different roles within the organization. Keep both the present and *our career* in mind as you engage with your employer. Give some thought to what you would like to discuss with your manager. Use The CARE Code as a framework for this discussion. Here are some questions to consider for your conversations:

- What type of career experiences will be most useful for you?

- How can you develop and grow as a professional? For example, stretch assignments, short-term projects, developmental assignments, secondments.

- Discuss options to give you increased visibility within the organization.

- Discuss the possibility of an international assignment if this will help you in your career trajectory. Keep in mind the locations and timing that you agreed on with your partner. Use this information to best position yourself to be offered a location of choice for you and your partner.

Chapter 6

How Organizations Can CARE

In this chapter you will learn:

- Why organizations need to care.
- Why the old model of talent management does not work.
- How organizations can CARE.

The focus up to now has been on the Dual Career Couple as they have their CARE Conversations. But no man is an island. Once the couple have had their CARE Conversations, they need to talk to other key stakeholders, the primary one being the organization they work for. But are organizations aware of the dilemma facing Dual Career Couples? Have they considered whether their current model for international assignments is truly effective in retaining talent? And even if they are aware of the dilemma for both couples and the organization, do they know how to address it?

What Can We Learn from Research?

- **International assignments.** Industry figures show the following (see *Chapters 2* and *3*): (i) partner resistance is the main reason for assignment refusal, and (ii) failure of partner and/or family to adjust to the new location is the main reason for assignment failure. It is curious that industry has grappled with this phenomenon for at least the last 30 years without coming up with a satisfactory solution. At best, companies offer the Accompanying Partner assistance with career advice (62%), intercultural and/or language training (51%) and job search assistance (45%). But this has not fixed the problem, as reflected in a 2019 Employment Conditions Abroad (ECA) article, which says that prior to assignment abroad, 79% of partners are in paid employment and 10% are self-employed. But while on assignment, only 28% work for an organization, 7% are self-employed and 65% are not working at all. The Permits Foundation Survey of 2013 shows that 80% of partners who were working in the host location reported its positive impact on their health and well-being. Furthermore, 55% of them reported that they were willing to consider another international assignment compared to 41% of non-working partners. These survey results provide a compelling argument as to why organizations cannot continue to adopt a business-as-usual approach. They need to take another look at their talent management strategy for Dual Career Couples. As the importance of career to both partners increases, meeting this need will become crucial and challenging for organizations.

- **Growth in Dual Career Couples.** The number of Dual Career Couples is growing globally. Assortative mating has risen 25% in the last 30 years and continues to increase. Today, 78% of millennials are Dual Career Couples. The McKinsey report 'Making it Work: How Dual-Career Couples Find Career Fulfillment' points out that Dual Career Couples experience a "tug of war" between the conflicting demands of work/home and their partner's career. Failure to deal with the joint ambitions of couples will result in a failure to attract and retain talent, attain gender parity and maintain employee engagement and well-being.

- **Impact of women at senior levels.** Research looking at the impact of having more women in the C-suite found that:
  - Firms become more open to change and less open to risk.
  - The top management becomes more focused on balancing

innovation with risk mitigation.
o Firms frequently shift their focus from M&A to R&D and consider a variety of value creation strategies.
o Leadership teams with more women are more balanced, collaborative and have a broader view of how to manage large, complex organizations.

This shows that organizations will clearly benefit from having more women in leadership and senior management roles. However, research indicates that this is not happening.

The 2020 analysis by Mercer of 1,100 organizations shows that the number of women decreases the further up the corporate ladder one goes. Only 23% of executives are women, whereas at support staff level, 47% are women. International assignments are a career accelerator and often women refuse such opportunities because of concerns for their partner's career.

o Globally, approximately 29% of senior management roles were held by women in 2020.
o The EY and NetExpat Relocating Partner Survey Report (2018) showed that only 29% of mobile employees were women.

Therefore, if we hope to close the gender gap at senior management level, organizations will need to do more to proactively manage international assignments as a strategy for improved diversity. CARE Conversations between employers and employees become imperative.

• **How men and women approach their careers.** Women generally consider the careers of their partners to be of equal importance to theirs. Robin Ely and her colleagues in their survey of Harvard Business School graduates found that "more than half the men in Generation X and the Baby Boom said that when they left HBS, they expected that their careers would take priority over their spouses' or partners'… The vast majority of women anticipated that their careers would rank equally with their partners'." You may argue that it is a generational difference. But as you may remember, this same survey showed that even today, "Half of millennial men expect their careers to take precedence over their partners'. Only a quarter of millennial women expect their partners' careers to take precedence."

When the opportunity for an international assignment arises, all too often women assume automatically that they have to follow. So much so, that one female expatriate partner coined the term 'professional follower' for such people: those who used to have a professional career but, for many reasons, decided to leave their job and follow their partner.

Women are generally more concerned about what will happen to their partner's career. Therefore, companies need to take steps to encourage women to accept international assignments and proactively try to address the concerns they have. CARE Conversations that provide a forum for honest discussion and for exploring options for the partner would be a vital first step. Women should also be invited to have CARE Conversations with their partners if they haven't had one before.

- **Broader focus of the current global workforce.** Reports show that the global workforce is currently comprised of 35% millennials and 24% Generation Z. Increasingly, work is about more than wages; the younger members of the workforce are more motivated by non-financial rewards like trust, recognition and alignment with company values. Employee well-being is an important driver for value creation. According to human capital specialists, when employees feel happier at work, they are more engaged, more productive, more creative and negotiate better on behalf of the company.

Meet Clara

Clara had decided years ago that she wanted to have time for her baby as well as her career. To achieve this, she joined a company that had family-friendly policies, and, more importantly, a company that would not stigmatize her for leaving punctually to be home for bedtime. She chose to work for this company precisely because it was 'mother-friendly.' Clara is a high performer, greatly valued for her leadership skills and astute business savvy. Headhunters contact her frequently. She has had opportunities to move to rival companies that offered her substantial salary increases. But she opts to stay here because of its family-friendly policies and lack of stigmatization.

Stories such as this show clearly that it makes business sense to care – because it increases talent retention, employee engagement and well-being, which in turn improves performance and hence profits for the company.

To sum up, research clearly indicates that talent, generally female talent, is being lost for a variety of reasons. What may have been a successful model for international assignments in the past is no longer the best approach for today's Dual Career Couples.

Why Is the Old Model Not Working?

Current talent management systems are designed with just the employee in mind. Assumptions were made that the partner would 'trail.' Hence the term "trailing spouse," first used by Mary Bralove in an article for *The Wall Street Journal* titled 'Problems of

Two-Career Families Start Forcing Businesses to Adapt' in 1981. This is how one spouse describes her Dual Career experience: "I think the whole system and process is designed for one partner to be 'trailing.'" Even the move itself assumes that someone is always at hand to manage logistics/dependents while the working partner gets right back to work. This approach no longer works; organizations have to adopt a fit-for-purpose approach that meets the needs of an increasing number of Dual Career Couples.

Organizations may be supporting spouses, but the numbers paint a stark reality. The Relocating Partner Survey Final Report (2019) shows that 90% of employers offer spousal support to their relocating families and yet the ECA reports that only approximately 35% of spouses are working. Other surveys conducted by individual organizations show that 90% of respondents want to work while accompanying their spouses. The reality is that Accompanying Partners are finding it increasingly difficult to find employment.

To compound this issue, the top decision makers in many companies are boomers who hold very traditional views about career prioritization. They find it difficult to understand why Dual Career Couples are dissatisfied when the package for an international assignment appears so generous. Worse still, many companies expect talented managers to move at the drop of a hat. Others expect their high potentials to gain exposure to company operations by rotating through three roles in three geographic locations. Jennifer Petriglieri in her article on 'Talent Management and the Dual-Career Couple' suggests that "the crux of the problem is that companies tend to have fixed paths to leadership roles, with set tours of duty and long-held ideas about what ambitions look like." No thought is given to the impact of such an approach on Dual Career Couples.

Many couples report being stigmatized for trying to negotiate greater flexibility with mobility. This often results in the loss of talent to more accommodating, forward-thinking competitors.

It is therefore evident that the organization has to rethink its talent management strategy for Dual Career Couples in order to retain its best talent and maximize the value that Dual Career Couples can bring to the organization.

What Can Organizations Do?

The long-term solution lies in the rethinking of the talent management of Dual Career Couples. As Jennifer Petriglieri points out in her aforementioned article, "Designing effective leadership-development paths for dual-career couples requires two changes: a revised notion of what is needed to achieve growth and advancement, and a shift in the organizational culture to embrace flexibility in the talent development process." Culture change takes time and buy-in from top management, which is not within the scope of this book. However, in the meantime, there are a few key changes that could make a difference to talent attraction and retention, as well as increase employee engagement.

Here I suggest three approaches employers could consider:

1. Treat the Dual Career Couple as one entity

Despite the well-known adage 'happy wife, happy life,' organizations still forget to engage with the partner, who often holds the key to whether the high potential employee or critical talent that is needed at location x will be willing to relocate. Even today, many companies view a partner's reluctance to move for career reasons as a private matter for the couple to solve. Except that their decision can have a negative impact on the talent flow.

HR and managers can start thinking of Dual Career Couples as *one entity* and assume that both careers matter; in other words, they need to recognize that both partners would like to work while on assignment. With the increase in assortative mating, many Accompanying Partners are extremely well qualified. For example, approximately 60% of Accompanying Partners of staff in international organizations have master's degrees. Thus, Accompanying Partners want to be employed in positions that enable them to make good use of their current skills and, hopefully, develop new skills. The current concern is that the Accompanying Partner is underemployed and thus dissatisfied. Spousal support, therefore, needs to provide real job opportunities in roles that add to their career skills.

Hence, employers could try to match mobility options to the needs of the Dual Career Couple, instead of forcing the couple to make a choice between *yours* and *mine*. Increasingly, Dual Career Couples are not willing to make the trade-off. At the very least, organizations need to factor into the mobility equation the fact that the partner is a key stakeholder. Here is where organizations too can use The CARE Code as a structure for having career conversations with future or current leaders about where and when to move.

2. Planning and policies

Evidence shows that Dual Career Couples are generally willing to move because of one partner's job. They appreciate that if they aspire to senior roles, this requires moving across functions and geographies. But they are unwilling to move at a moment's notice or at an inopportune time in their partner's equally important career. They are not willing to choose between *yours* and *mine*. Often that refusal is interpreted by the organization as a lack of ambition, and they are not offered such good opportunities again. This frequently leads to a loss of talent as they begin to look for employers who are more willing to accommodate their life priorities. Many indicate that they are willing to go, provided it is a deliberate, planned career move.

Advance planning, to the extent possible, and a transparent conversation can clarify to the talented employee what his/her long-term prospects might be and how they can be achieved. A key element is to align the organization's plans with the employee's situation as one partner of a Dual Career Couple.

Of course, organizations have policies that cover international assignments. But do these have to be rigidly applied or is there some flexibility? For example, *turn-taking* is a good career prioritization model (see Case Study 1). Instead of back-to-back assignments, allow couples to return to a 'home base' to allow the Accompanying Partner to recalibrate his/her career or return to a new role after a leave of absence. A less rigid approach to the length of assignments will also help Dual Career Couples; thus, instead of a four-year assignment, consider two years, as the Accompanying Partner may only be able to get a two-year leave of absence.

In addition to short-term and commuter assignments, new policies can be introduced to increase flexibility for the Dual Career Couple. In the wake of Covid-19, we have all come to understand how effective remote working is. How can organizations bring this into their policies for international assignments?

A combination of planning and policies can help to solve career prioritization, which is a key dilemma Dual Career Couples face (see *Chapter 4*). By showing flexibility with assignment planning and modifying their policies, organizations can help to solve this dilemma and reduce the possibility of losing talent.

3. Use The CARE Code for career conversations

HR specialists will have formal opportunities to engage with the organization's talented staff, while line managers can have both formal and informal discussions with their direct reports. The formal route for managers will be via performance review conversations, where growth and career development conversations take place. HR specialists need to provide more specific details about international assignments and the possibilities of employment for the Accompanying Partner.

These conversations must be used as opportunities to CARE (Clarify, Assess, Refocus and Explore) and discuss career experiences that can be mutually beneficial for the organization and the couple. The HR specialist or line manager needs to keep in mind both the organization's business needs and the employee's concerns. Achieving the right balance is not easy, and so where line managers have these conversations with top talent, they should receive training from HR on how to conduct them.

The CARE Code can be used by HR specialists and/or line managers to co-create a win-win solution. But a win-win can only be achieved when transparency and honesty pervade the conversation. For example, creating false expectations will lead to insuperable difficulties in the future. The prerequisites for The CARE Code to work effectively are trust and psychological safety.

Here are some suggestions on how to use The CARE Code.

1. Clarify

HR specialist/line manager:
- Clarify where the employee is in his/her career and how the organization plans to harness his/her potential.
- Provide details on any planned international assignments with realistic timelines.

- Learn what matters to the employee as an individual and as a partner of a Dual Career Couple.
- Encourage the employee to have an exploratory CARE conversation with his/her partner.

2. Assess

HR specialist/line manager:

- Assess the barriers or challenges that the couple may be facing.
- Make sure you understand the employee's dilemma that is being discussed.
- Discuss what the organization can do and how it can be flexible.

3. Refocus

HR specialist/line manager:

- Decide together what the issues are for both parties (organization and couple) and where you need to refocus.
- Rethink how the organization can be more Dual Career friendly.

4. Explore

HR specialist/line manager:

- Explore the options and opportunities that are available to both the couple and the organization.
- Arrange a follow-up discussion with the results of the exploration to show that you care.

Chapter 7

Conclusion: Keeping Your Focus on CARE

Staying on Track

This book has offered some useful strategies to make your Dual Career and mobile lifestyle work in alignment with your priorities. It has also provided a framework to guide your discussions as a couple and your career conversations with your organization. But one key question arises: How can we stay on track?

Graham and I have found, over three decades of our Dual Career journey, that keeping the communication lines open, keeping the four horsemen out of our relationship and making shared decisions have kept us on track.

There will always be bumps in the road of life, but if you are to stay on track, you must have regular Dual Career Conversations. Such conversations will be about what matters to you both at this point in time and how you can support each other in achieving the life you both desire. You must also make shared decisions and respect the no-go zones and priorities you have agreed on. These are the Three Key Golden Rules that we have already discussed in *Chapter 5*, but because you must never stop doing these three things, I like to call them the Three CARE Habits.

The Three CARE Habits

1. Have regular Dual Career Conversations.

2. Respect each other's no-go zones.

3. Make shared decisions.

Each of our Case Studies clearly demonstrates that the success of their Dual Career management was because the couples made CARE Conversations a regular part of their lives and because all their career decisions were shared decisions. The Three CARE Habits will make the difference to your own Dual Careers.

The couples in the Case Studies reported that ongoing conversations became more intense if one or both partners were facing career challenges, such as mid-career transition, a prospective move or an unexpected career opportunity. Times like these require both renegotiation and recalibration, particularly as we move through different life stages and circumstances. Use these occasions as prompts to revisit what matters most to the both of you. For example, Robert and Rosemary's oldest child (see Case Study 1) will start middle school in two years' time; they are already starting to think about where they want the children to attend high school and university, as this will give them time to position their careers for the future.

CARE Makes It Work

Keep practicing these Three CARE Habits and following The CARE Code of Clarify, Assess, Refocus and Explore to regularly revisit both your *priorities* and your *no-go zones*. This will help you navigate new, unknown and unchartered waters.

The same applies if you are going through a difficult time and think you may have gone off track. Don't be discouraged. Go back to the basics and use The CARE Code to identify where the problem lies and then to refocus. It will be helpful to go through the exercises again to remind yourself of your priorities and to assess what went wrong. The results will form the basis for regular, in-depth discussions with your partner and a new round of shared decisions.

Jennifer Petriglieri, author of *Couples That Work*, interviewed 113 Dual Career Couples aged 26 to 63 from 32 different countries to try to answer the questions *Is combining love and work a more complex, relational ongoing effort?* and *How do two careers combine over time?* She discovered that the couples who reported that they felt successful in both their careers and their relationship had one thing in common: "They had all explicitly discussed and agreed on how to prioritize their careers, rather than leaving the issue unexplored and unresolved." They were deliberate in addressing the question *How do we make this work?*

The Case Studies in *Chapter 4, A Win for All*, corroborate her research findings. Each Case Study reflects a different career prioritization model. The common weave of their success lies in adopting the Three CARE Habits.

The post-Covid world of work is opening up more options for short-term assignments, commuter assignments and working remotely (which means working from home). It may solve the problem of careers for Dual Career Couples because there could be fewer international relocations. But it offers a different set of problems – solo parenting, for example. The question *How do we make this work?* still needs to be addressed. Use The CARE Code in your conversations; it is a tool to help couples co-design 'OUR' future.

"One day you will tell your story of how you've overcome what you are going through now, and it will become part of someone else's survival guide," says Ehraz Ahmed, Founder and CEO of Aspirehive. My hope is that this book in some way has contributed to your survival guide. Or better still, it will become your 'how to flourish' manual.

QUICK REFERENCE GUIDE

The Eight Golden Rules

GOLDEN RULE #1: SHARE CAREER UPS AND DOWNS WITH YOUR PARTNER; IT'S NOT 'YOURS' AND 'MINE' – IT'S 'OURS'

GOLDEN RULE #2: MAKE SHARED DECISIONS

GOLDEN RULE #3: SET YOUR 'NO-GO' AREAS EARLY ON

GOLDEN RULE #4: BE EQUALLY INVESTED IN EACH OTHER'S CAREER

GOLDEN RULE #5: MAKE DUAL CAREER CONVERSATIONS A HABIT

GOLDEN RULE #6: THOROUGHLY RESEARCH EMPLOYMENT OPPORTUNITIES IN THE NEW LOCATION BEFORE YOU GO

GOLDEN RULE #7: AGREE ON THE PARAMETERS FOR POSSIBLE ASSIGNMENTS

GOLDEN RULE #8: A WIN FOR ONE MUST BE EXPERIENCED AS A WIN FOR ALL

The Twelve Common Pitfalls

PITFALL #1: LETTING YOUR CAREER COME SECOND TOO EASILY

PITFALL #2: MAKING DO WITH WHAT IS AT HAND RATHER THAN FOCUSING ON YOUR CAREER PATH

PITFALL #3: SOON YOUR TWO CAREERS ARE OUT OF SYNC

PITFALL #4: COMPETING PRIORITIES GET IN THE WAY

PITFALL #5: YOU READILY AGREE TO FOLLOW BECAUSE YOU ARE CURRENTLY NOT VESTED IN YOUR OWN CAREER

PITFALL #6: YOU DON'T TAKE SUFFICIENT TIME TO THINK ABOUT THE IMPLICATIONS OF THE MOVE FOR YOU

PITFALL #7: YOU DON'T DISCUSS YOUR CAREER CONTINUITY AND COORDINATION, WHICH LEADS TO ONE PARTNER HAVING TO 'STOP AND START' WITH EACH MOVE

PITFALL #8: YOU DON'T FIND OUT ENOUGH INFORMATION ABOUT YOUR PARTNER'S PLANNED MOVE

PITFALL #9: YOU UNDERESTIMATE THE COST

PITFALL #10: YOU DON'T GET INFORMATION ABOUT THE LOCAL EMPLOYMENT MARKET IN RELATION TO YOUR SKILLS

PITFALL #11: YOU DON'T FULLY UNDERSTAND THE UNINTENDED CONSEQUENCES OF ROLE REVERSAL

PITFALL #12: YOU ASSUME THAT YOUR ROLE IS TO FOLLOW AND THAT YOUR CAREER IS AUTOMATICALLY THE SECONDARY ONE

The CARE Code

Use The CARE Code To Solve Dual Career Dilemmas

C **A** **R** **E**

Step One:	Step Two:	Step Three:	Step Four:
Clarify	**A**ssess	**R**efocus	**E**xplore

Clarify

- Decide on what matters to you individually and as a couple.

- Agree on the priorities for your careers and life together.

- Communicate regularly.

Assess

- Agree on no-go zones.

- Anticipate challenges that may arise.

- Make shared decisions.

Refocus

- Listen attentively to each other.

- Respect no-go zones.

- Repair as needed.

Explore

- Research thoroughly your options and check assumptions.

- Proactively partner with each other, your organization and other significant stakeholders.

- Take action.

The Three CARE Habits

1. Have regular Dual Career Conversations.

2. Respect each other's no-go zones.

3. Make shared decisions.

RESOURCES

Introduction

'Relocating Partner Survey Report' (2018). EY and NetExpat: https://work-live-stay.dk/foreningenwls/wp-content/uploads/2019/09/ey-2018-relocating-partner-survey-final-report.pdf

Chapter 1

Petriglieri, J. (2019). *Couples That Work: How Dual Career Couples Can Thrive in Love and Work*, Harvard Business Review

Chapter 2

Websites and articles

Duport, P. 'It's my job. Expatriate women often overlook their careers', *Radio France*, May 2017: https://www.francetvinfo.fr/replay-radio/c-est-mon-boulot/c-est-mon-boulot-les-femmes-d-expatries-font-souvent-une-croix-sur-leur-carriere_2195604.html

'Talent Management for Dual-Career Expatriate Couples', *Strategic Advisor*, Brookfield Global Relocation Services, Vol. 11 No. 111, June 2015: https://expatresearch.com/files/1714/3458/6351/06-05_Brookfield_June_15.pdf

Orgad, S. ''Wifehood' is not old-fashioned – here's why it matters', Oct 2018: https://theconversation.com/wifehood-is-not-old-fashioned-heres-why-it-matters-103947

van Gils, W., & Kraaykamp, G. (2008). 'The Emergence of the Dual Career Couples: A Longitudinal Study of the Netherlands', *International Sociology*, 23, 345–366

Känsälä, M., Mäkelä, L., & Suutari, V. (2015). 'Career coordination strategies among dual career expatriate couples', *The International Journal of Human Resource Management*, 26(17), 2187–2210: https://dx.doi.org/10.1080/09585192.2014.985327

Shaffer, M. A., & Harrison, D. A. (2001). 'Forgotten partners of international assignments: Development and test of a model of spouse adjustment', *Journal of Applied Psychology*, 86(2), 238–254: https://psycnet.apa.org/ doiLanding?doi=10.1037%2F0021-9010.86.2.238

Weir, K. (2020, Jun). 'Grieving life and loss', *American Psychological Association*, 51(4): https://www.apa.org/monitor/2020/06/covid-grieving-life

'Work authorization for family members. Global summary of country regulations' (2019), Permits Foundation: https://www.permitsfoundation.com/wp-content/uploads/ 2019/07/Global-summary-work-authorisation-family-members-July-2019.pdf

Books

Orgad, S. (2019). *Heading Home: Motherhood, Work, and the Failed Promise of Equality*, Columbia University Press

Surveys

'Relocating Partner Survey Report' (2018). EY and NetExpat:

https://work-live-stay.dk/foreningenwls/wp-content/uploads/
2019/09/ey-2018-relocating-partner-survey-final-report.pdf

'From Expat Lab Barometer: 2019 results' (2019). Expat
Communication:
https://www.expatcommunication.com/expat-lab/expat-lab-
barometer-2019-results

'Expat Insider 2019 Business Edition: A Look at Global Talent
Mobility Through Expat Eyes' (2019). Internations Business
Solutions:
https://cms-internationsgmbh.netdna-ssl.com/cdn/file/cms-
media/public/2019-09/Expat-Insider-2019_The-InterNations-
Survey_0.pdf

'International Survey Summary Report, Second Edition' (2013),
Permits Foundation:
https://www.permitsfoundation.com/wp-content/uploads/
2013/04/Spousal-survey-new-style.pdf

'International Mobility and Dual Career Survey of International
Employers' (2012). Permits Foundation:
https://www.permitsfoundation.com/wp-content/uploads/
2013/04/Permits-Global-Employers-Survey-2012.pdf

Chapter 3

Websites and articles

Schiebinger, L., Henderson, A., & Gilmartin, S. (2008). *Dual-
Career Academic Couples: What Universities Need to Know*,
Michelle R. Clayman Institute for Gender Research, Stanford

Ely, R. J., Stone, P., & Ammerman, C. (2014, Dec). 'Rethink What You 'Know' About High-Achieving Women', *Harvard Business Review*:
https://hbr.org/2014/12/rethink-what-you-know-about-high-achieving-women

Cole, N. (2012). 'Expatriate Accompanying Partners: The males speak', *Asia Pacific Journal of Human Resources*, 50(3), 308–326

Groysberg, B., & Abrahams, R. (2015). 'Marriage and the Marketplace: Dual-Career Couples in the 21st Century', working paper:
https://www.hbs.edu/faculty/Pages/item.aspx?num=48720

Forret, M., Sullivan, S., & Mainiero, L. (2010). 'Gender role differences in reactions to unemployment: Exploring psychological mobility and boundaryless careers', *Journal of Organizational Behavior*, 31, 647–666

Känsälä, M., Mäkelä, L. and Suutari, V. (2015), 'Career coordination strategies among dual career expatriate couples', *The International Journal of Human Resource Management*, 26 (17), 2187–2210:
https://dx.doi.org/10.1080/09585192.2014.985327

van Gils, W., & Kraaykamp, G. (2008). 'The Emergence of the Dual Career Couples: A Longitudinal Study of the Netherlands', *International Sociology*, 23, 345–366

McNulty, Y. (2012). 'Being dumped to sink or swim: An empirical study of organizational support for the trailing spouse', *Human Resource Development International*, 15(4): 417–434

"Wifehood' is not old-fashioned – here's why it matters', Shai Orgad, Oct 2018:
https://theconversation.com/wifehood-is-not-old-fashioned-heres-why-it-matters-103947

Books

Orgad, S. (2019). *Heading Home: Motherhood, Work, and the Failed Promise of Equality*, Columbia University Press

Gray, J. (2012). *Men Are from Mars, Women Are from Venus*, Harper

Surveys

'Relocating Partner Survey Report' (2018). EY and NetExpat:
https://work-live-stay.dk/foreningenwls/wp-content/uploads/2019/09/ey-2018-relocating-partner-survey-final-report.pdf

'Expat Insider 2019 Business Edition: A Look at Global Talent Mobility Through Expat Eyes'_(2019). Internations Business Solutions:
https://cms-internationsgmbh.netdna-ssl.com/cdn/file/cms-media/public/2019-09/Expat-Insider-2019_The-InterNations-Survey_0.pdf

Michielsen, A. 'How best to support partners on assignment?', *ECA International*, February 2019:
https://www.eca-international.com/insights/blog/february-2019/how-best-to-support-partners-on-assignment

Chapter 4

Books

Pfeffer, J. (2010). *Power: Why Some People Have it – And others Don't*, Harper Business

Quahe, Y. (1986). *We Remember: Cameos of Pioneer Life*, Landmark

Hoffman, R., & Casnocha, B. (2012). *The Start-Up of You: Adapt to the Future, Invest in Yourself, and Transform Your Career*, Cornerstone Digital

Chapter 5

Websites and articles

Ryan, R. 'Autonomy, Competence and Relatedness', Center for Self-Determination Theory: https://selfdeterminationtheory.org/application-basic-psychological-needs/

Beutel, E. 'Landmark Study on 11,196 Couples Pinpoints What Dating Apps Get So Wrong', *Inverse*, July 2020: https://www.inverse.com/mind-body/dating-study-predicts-happy-relationships

Kaur, M. 'Want Stronger Relationships at Work? Change the Way You Listen', *Harvard Business Review*, July 2020: https://hbr.org/2020/07/want-stronger-relationships-at-work-change-the-way-you-listen

Wells, M. 'The Five C's – 5 Keys to Communication for Couples', *Marriage.com*, March 2020:
https://www.marriage.com/advice/communication/keys-to-communication-for-couples/

Lisitsa, E. 'The Four Horsemen: Criticism, Contempt, Defensiveness, and Stonewalling', *The Gottman Institute*, April 2013:
https://www.gottman.com/blog/the-four-horsemen-recognizing-criticism-contempt-defensiveness-and-stonewalling/

Benson, K. 'The Magic Relationship Ratio, According to Science', *The Gottman Institute*, October 2017:
https://www.gottman.com/blog/the-magic-relationship-ratio-according-science/

Laurence, E. '5 Things the Happiest Couples Have in Common, According to Over 11,000 Long-Term Relationships', September 2020:
https://www.wellandgood.com/secrets-relationships/

Mohn, T. 'Plight of the Expat Spouse', *New York Times*, June 2011:
https://www.nytimes.com/2011/06/21/business/21expats.html

'What are the HALT Risk States?', *Mind Tools*:
https://www.mindtools.com/pages/article/HALT-risk-states.htm

Making It Work: How Dual-Career Couples Find Career Fulfillment, McKinsey & Co:
https://www.mckinsey.com/business-functions/organization/our-insights/how-dual-career-couples-find-fulfillment-at-work#

Ely, R. J., Stone, P., & Ammerman, C. 'Rethink What You 'Know' About High-Achieving Women', *Harvard Business Review*, December 2014: https://hbr.org/2014/12/rethink-what-you-know-about-high-achieving-women

Wittenberg-Cox, A. 'Being a Two-Career Couple Requires a Long-Term Plan', *Harvard Business Review*, February 2018: https://hbr.org/2018/02/being-a-two-career-couple-requires-a-long-term-plan

Books

Quahe, Y. (1986). *We Remember: Cameos of Pioneer Life*, Landmark

Petriglieri, J. (2019). *Couples That Work: How Dual Career Couples Can Thrive in Love and Work*, Harvard Business Review

Chapter 6

Websites and articles

Bralove, M. 'Problems of Two-Career Families Start Forcing Businesses to Adapt', *Wall Street Journal*, July 1981

Ely, R. J., Stone, P., & Ammerman, C. 'Rethink What You 'Know' About High-Achieving Women', *Harvard Business Review*, December 2014: https://hbr.org/2014/12/rethink-what-you-know-about-high-achieving-women

'Women in Management: Quick Take', *Catalyst*, August 2020: https://www.catalyst.org/research/women-in-management/

Post, C., Lokshin, B., & Boone, C. 'Adding Women to the C-Suite Changes How Companies Think', *Harvard Business Review*, April 2021:
https://hbr.org/2021/04/research-adding-women-to-the-c-suite-changes-how-companies-think

Petriglieri, J. 'Talent Management and the Dual-Career Couple', *Harvard Business Review*, May–June 2018:
https://hbr.org/2018/05/talent-management-and-the-dual-career-couple

Michielsen, A. 'How best to support partners on assignment?', *ECA International*, February 2019:
https://www.eca-international.com/insights/blog/february-2019/how-best-to-support-partners-on-assignment

Meier, O. 'The Path to Diversity: Women on Assignment', *Mercer*:
https://mobilityexchange.mercer.com/Insights/article/The-Path-to-Diversity-Women-on-Assignment

Books

Petriglieri, J. (2019). *Couples That Work: How Dual Career Couples Can Thrive in Love and Work*, Harvard Business Review

Surveys and reports

Making It Work: How Dual-Career Couples Find Career Fulfillment, McKinsey & Co:
https://www.mckinsey.com/business-functions/organization/our-insights/how-dual-career-couples-find-fulfillment-at-work

'How to improve gender diversity in the expat workplace?', *Allianz*, June 2019:

https://www.allianzcare.com/en/employers/employer-blogs/
2019/06/gender-diversity.html

'Barometer 2017: White Paper – Graphics', Expat
Communication:
https://www.expatcommunication.com/expat-lab/global-
survey-2017

'Managing International Assignments', SHRM:
https://www.shrm.org/resourcesandtools/tools-and-samples/
toolkits/pages/cms_010358.aspx
'Relocating Partner Survey Report' (2018). EY and NetExpat:
https://work-live-stay.dk/foreningenwls/wp-content/uploads/
2019/09/ey-2018-relocating-partner-survey-final-report.pdf

Useful Online Resources

Chowdhury, M. R. 'The 3 Best Questionnaires for Measuring
Values', *Positive Psychology*, April 2021:
https://positivepsychology.com/values-questionnaire/

Use the cutting-edge personality *test values* finder to get insights
about your personal *values* and to act in congruence with them:
https://findyourvalues.com/

Work *values* are crucial to career success and job satisfaction.
Take this *free* work *values test online*. What work *values* do you
value most?
https://www.123test.com/work-values-test/

If you feel in need of professional help, the best online marriage
counseling programs:
https://www.verywellmind.com/best-online-marriage-
counseling-4691952

Books

Bradley, B., & Furrow, J. (2013). *Emotionally Focused Couple Therapy for Dummies*, For Dummies

Bridges, W. (2004). *Transitions: Making Sense of Life's Changes*, Da Capo

Iyenga, S. (2011). *The Art of Choosing*, Twelve

Johnson, S. (2008). *Hold Me Tight: Seven Conversations for a Lifetime of Love*, Little, Brown Spark

Kallos-Lilly, V., & Fitzgerald, J. (2014). *An Emotionally Focused Workbook for Couples: The Two of Us*, Routledge

Petriglieri, J. (2019). *Couples That Work: How Dual Career Couples Can Thrive in Love and Work*, Harvard Business Review

Acknowledgments

My grateful thanks to each and every one of you who have made a unique and valuable contribution to this book.

First things first, to our Great Matchmaker who brought us together.

My spouse, Graham, who refused to be named as co-author. Without you, none of this would have been possible. You have been my editor, sounding board, my strength and stay. You kept me going when I was ready to throw it all in. You hold on and hold me when I am ready to let go. This is as much yours as it is mine.

Our son, Alastair, for his incisive comments and support. Our daughter, Antonia, for her support and being at the other end of WhatsApp.

Ruth Van Reken who birthed the first iteration of the table of contents with me and told me to contact Jo Parfitt. Jo, little did you know what you were getting into! Thank you for your patience and guidance in getting this book to publication and for being the pioneer that you are.

Robert and Rosemary, Melissa and Christian, Maja and Henrik, Amanda and Simon, Cielo and Charles, Chuck and Chen. You know who you are; thank you for your candor and willingness to share your journey as a Dual Career Couple.

The numerous Accompanying Partners I have met both professionally and personally; your stories are the reason I have felt compelled to write.

Yvonne Kallane (McNulty), your research has been a pivotal influence on my thinking and research. Thank you for writing the foreword and for never letting being an Accompanying Partner stop you from achieving your career goals.

Lesley Lewis, Rachel Cason, thank you for the contributing exercises that can be found on my website www.yvonnequahe.com.

Catherine Mathieu, for inviting me to design the Career Lab, which turned out to be a gold mine of research and a source of inspiration. Thank you for your unyielding support.

My beta readers, Ginny Philps, Shalu Rajesh Advani, Ashikur Rahman, Rebekah Magnano, Jose Deduque and Venice Mascarinas for your thoughtful feedback and comments. Thank you.

My cheering squad, you have encouraged me, cheered me on, inquired after my progress, shared your stories and your connections, urged me to write and are now waiting to read my book. Thank you.

About the Author

Yvonne Quahe is Singaporean by birth, a sociologist by training, a facilitator, coach, HR professional and author.

She has walked in the shoes of her clients, having lived abroad as a working professional and accompanying partner in Hong Kong, Singapore, the Philippines, the UK and now the USA. While experiencing the challenges and rewards of being part of a Dual Career Couple in a bicultural marriage, Yvonne is also mother to two third culture children who changed schools three times. Professionally, she is passionate about helping individuals manage their careers by providing results-focused coaching, which harnesses their brains to improve the quality of their career and life. She has expertise in challenging and supporting clients as they navigate change and career dilemmas and is an ardent advocate of helping Dual Career women find their voice.

Yvonne has spent the last 13 years of her career designing and developing programs for Dual Career families in support of the World Bank Group's efforts to facilitate talent mobility. She is currently the Career and Program Advisor at the World Bank Group Family Network. In 2017 she designed the Career Lab to address the challenges faced by accompanying partners. She is also the author of the book *We Remember: Cameos of Pioneer Life*, a social history of Singapore using oral history as a medium of documentation. She also speaks at international conferences, panel discussions, podcasts and talk shows.

You can connect with Yvonne at the following:

e: yvonne@yvonnequahe.com
w: www.yvonnequahe.com
l: https://www.linkedin.com/in/yvonne-quahe-6083ab32/

book design by

www.
CREATIONBOOTH
.COM

www.ingramcontent.com/pod-product-compliance
Lightning Source LLC
Chambersburg PA
CBHW070929030426
42336CB00014BA/2594